THE END OF
THE SEARCH

THE END OF THE SEARCH

Discovery and Encounter
with the Divine

Marchette Chute

I-Level
Acropolis Books, Publisher
Lakewood, Colorado

THE END OF THE SEARCH
Discovery and Encounter
with the Divine

First Acropolis Books Edition 1998

Published by Acropolis Books
under its *I*-Level imprint

Printed in the United States of America.

Acropolis Books, Inc.
Lakewood, Colorado

6|q 9

http://www.acropolisbooks.com

————·►◄·————

Cover design by Bren Frisch

Library Of Congress Cataloging-In-Publication Data

Chute, Marchette Gaylord, 1909–
    The end of the search: discovery and encounter with the Divine /
Marchette Chute. — 1st Acropolis Books ed.
        p.   cm.
    Originally published: New York : North River Press, 1947
    Includes bibliographical references.
    ISBN 1-889051-28-4 (pbk. : alk. paper)
    1. Bible. N.T. Acts—Criticism, interpretation, etc. 2. Bible. N.T. Epistles—Criticism,
interpretation, etc. 3. Bible. N.T. Revelation—Criticism, interpretation, etc. 4. God—Biblical
teaching. 5. Desire for God—Biblical teaching.   I. Title.
BS2617.8.C48 1998
225.6—dc21   97–52672
                                                                                                        CIP

This book is printed on acid free paper that meets standard Z 39.48 of the
American National Standards Institute

TABLE OF CONTENTS

PART ONE

PART TWO

FOREWORD

This book is a sequel to *The Search For God* by the same author. It continues where the final chapter left off, and carries the discussion through the remaining books of the Bible.

The record of the Gospels closes when Jesus left his followers alone to carry on the search for truth by themselves. The rest of the New Testament records their efforts to obey his instructions.

It records in particular the activities of two men, Paul and John. Both were ardent seekers after God, but each man chose a different route. Paul chose an outward, John an inward way, and each man left a legacy behind him to help others in making a similar choice. Paul left a well-organized church, and John left the Book of Revelation.

M. C.

PART I

Note to The Reader

The translation used in Part I is from Smith and Goodspeed's *The Bible: An American Translation,* made by Edgar J. Goodspeed for the University of Chicago Press. It is a more accurate translation than the King James Version, since it mirrors the colloquial everyday diction used by the apostles themselves.

THE ACTS OF THE APOSTLES

We cannot help telling of what we have seen and heard.

Acts 4:20

T he early Christian church was composed of a group of men and women, about a hundred in all, who had seen Jesus alive after the crucifixion and who were convinced, for that reason, that he was the Messiah who had been promised. When they went out with the glory still upon them to tell this conviction to all Judea, they based their teaching squarely upon one fact and were willing to let their whole doctrine be tested by it alone. Jesus was the Messiah, or, in the Greek translation of the word, the Christ, because "death could not control him." (Acts 2:24)

"The Christ . . . was not deserted in death and his body was not destroyed. He is Jesus, whom God raised from the dead, and to whose resurrection we are all witnesses." (Acts 2:31–32) This was Peter's first public declaration, and out of the fire of his own certainty he made that morning about three thousand converts.

Peter assumed the leadership of the small group from the beginning, but otherwise there was no attempt at organization. There was no need. The whole group was of "one mind," as Luke called it, (Acts 1:14) and they needed no rules to hold them together. As long as the immediate glory of what they called the resurrection was still upon them they were united into a fellowship that could not be broken.

Luke is the historian of the period; and while in his preoccupation with angels he leaves something to be desired, he does succeed perfectly in communicating the spirit of the movement in its early days, the loving loyalty and happiness that bound together the small

1

group of Jews. "Everyone felt a sense of awe, and many signs and wonders were done by the apostles. The believers all shared everything they had with one another, and sold their property and belongings, and divided the money with all the rest, according to their special needs. Day after day they all went regularly to the temple, they broke their bread together in their homes, and they ate their food with glad and simple hearts, constantly praising God and respected by all the people." (Acts 2:43–47) The followers of this Messiah were no sect of wild-eyed visionaries; they were a group of sober Jewish citizens whose only peculiarity was that they loved each other and had found a reason for living.

If there had been no more than this to the doctrine they followed, it is possible they might have avoided conflict with the authorities, even though they proclaimed as the Messiah a man whom the authorities had executed. But Peter and John immediately found themselves in trouble with the upholders of established religion because they did what Jesus had told them to do. They healed the sick.

As the two men were going into the temple one day for afternoon prayer a lame beggar asked them for money. Peter and John stopped short and Peter said, "I have no silver or gold, but I will give you what I have. In the name of Jesus Christ of Nazareth, walk." (Acts 3:6) The man walked, to his own great astonishment and that of all the worshipers who were there at the time. A crowd began to gather around the three men in Solomon's Colonnade, and Peter at once raised his voice to explain what had happened. "Why do you stare at us so, as though it were some power or some piety of ours that had made him able to walk? . . . The God of our forefathers has done this honor to his servant Jesus . . . It is by his power and through faith in him that this man whom you see and recognize has been made strong again." (Acts 3:12–16)

John might have put this a little differently and called it God's power rather than that of Jesus. But John was always noticeably silent on these public occasions and as far as Peter was concerned Jesus was the central adoration of his life. His personal faith in Jesus had always been great, and after the resurrection it was irresistible. There was nothing the Lord Jesus could not do, and his servant Peter was prepared to prove it.

The healing of the crippled beggar had two results. The first was that Peter and John were arrested as dangerous characters, and the second was that the number of their followers almost doubled. The Sanhedrin was placed in a difficult position. They had not rid themselves of the false prophet by killing him; for his followers insisted that he had risen from the dead and they were multiplying so fast they constituted a real threat to the ecclesiastical authority that had killed their leader. Moreover, they shared the same awkward power of being able to prove what they said, for the beggar accompanied the prisoners into court and all Jerusalem knew that he had been a cripple from birth. The Sanhedrin failed in an effort to intimidate John and Peter and were reluctantly obliged to release them, since it was not technically a crime to heal a man inside the gates of the temple.

Matters grew steadily worse from the ecclesiastical point of view. Peter was almost worshiped by the populace "so that people would carry their sick out into the streets, and lay them down on beds and mats, to have at least Peter's shadow fall on some of them as he went by." (Acts 5:15) Finally all the leaders were again arrested by the harassed Council and showed such open defiance they narrowly escaped death. Their protector was a member of the Council named Gamaliel, who suggested privately to the Sanhedrin that the truth did not need their frenzied efforts to protect it. "If this idea or movement is of human origin it will come to naught, but if it is from God you will not be able to stop it. You may actually find yourselves fighting God." (Acts 5:38–39) This was so obviously true that his fellow-members could think of nothing with which to refute it; they flogged the men and then let them go.

The disciples had no intention of founding a new religion. All of them were Jews and completely loyal to the temple. Their only wish was to proclaim to Judea that the man who had been executed had risen from the dead and was therefore the promised Messiah. But the disciples discovered, as the number of their followers increased, that some kind of an organization was going to be inevitable. It had not been needed at the beginning, when their numbers were few and they were all bound together in the unconscious brotherhood of having known Jesus and having seen him after the resurrection. But as the movement gained in momentum and converts began to crowd into it, this spiritual union became less real and something more official had to be substituted.

The first indication that a set of rules was going to be necessary came early, when it became clear that the communal sharing of property, which had been so obvious and natural in the early days, began to be forced. One convert, fearful of public opinion and yet anxious to keep some of his money, shared part of his property and pretended he had shared it all, dying of sheer superstitious terror when the deception was found out. As Peter said, he had done a foolish thing, for the money was his own; but the case was the first sign that the original spirit of close harmony in the brotherhood was disappearing.

Almost at once there was another incident of the same kind. The Greek-speaking Jews lodged a complaint against the native Jews, charging that their widows were being neglected in the daily distribution of food. So jealous a watch over the distribution of food was inconsistent with the teachings of a man who had said, "Do not worry about life, wondering what you will have to eat or drink," (Matt. 6:25) and the disciples knew it. Yet there was nothing they could do except arrange a compromise. They remarked, with a certain irony, "It is not desirable that we should give up preaching the word of God to keep accounts," (Acts 6:2) but they arranged for the election of seven men, of known integrity to be put in charge of the distribution. The movement was obliged to organize itself, however loosely. It was no longer of "one mind."

One of these seven men was Stephen, the first of the martyrs. He had the kind of earnest, unquestioning faith that also belonged to Peter, and he did "remarkable signs and wonders among the people." (Acts 6:8) As in the case of Peter this was one thing the authorities could not tolerate, and they had Stephen arrested on the charge of having insulted Moses, the great giver of the Law.

Luke gives in full Stephen's speech in his own defense. He began with an orderly survey of Hebrew history, carrying his listeners over familiar ground so that they could not fail to agree with him. He reminded them of the well-known fact that Moses had been repudiated by his own followers, and then he suddenly stopped short to identify his judges with the same point of view that had repudiated Moses. "You are always opposing the holy Spirit, just as your forefathers did. Which of the prophets did your forefathers not persecute? They killed the men who foretold the coming of the righteous one whom you have now betrayed and killed—you who had the Law given to you by angels and did not obey it." (Acts 7:51–53)

To an impartial observer, Stephen's attitude toward the Law of Moses was less insulting than that of his accusers. But his judges were not impartial and under the circumstances could not be. They were determined to uproot the dangerous heresy which Stephen represented, and they handed him over to be stoned to death. Stephen went quietly, for his faith in Jesus was very great, and he died without a struggle and without fear. "Falling on his knees, he cried out, 'Lord, do not lay this sin up against them.' With these words he fell asleep." (Acts 7:60) Stephen's death was the signal for a wave of ecclesiastical persecution that scattered the small band over all Judea and Samaria and left the apostles almost alone.

The determined effort of the Sanhedrin to destroy the new religion was carried out by a young Pharisee named Saul, who had come up from Tarsus to learn the Law and was now prepared to protect it. Under Saul's tireless and efficient leadership the followers of the new doctrine were either imprisoned or driven out of Jerusalem. Not content with this, Saul asked permission to go to Damascus and search the Jewish synagogues there, so that he could complete successfully the work he had begun.

Saul set out for Damascus to destroy a dangerous sect that was threatening the existence of the Law. He arrived in the city with the Law forgotten, and with Saul in the grip of an experience so sudden and so complete that it reversed everything he had learned and made him an ardent convert to the movement he had set out to destroy. In one brief instant he abruptly forsook everything he had lived for, shaking it off like an old cloak, and accepted instead the "sudden light" (Acts 9:3) that threw him to the ground and nearly blinded him with its brilliance. In the lightning flash of that vision Saul the destroyer became Paul the apostle.

It took Paul a long time to assimilate what he had seen in that single moment of illumination, even though his life was dominated by it from that time forward. When he arrived in Damascus, half blinded, to be taken in by a member of the sect he had persecuted, he was sure of one thing only: that Jesus, whom his party had murdered, was the son of God he claimed to be. As soon as he was able, he went to proclaim that fact in the nearest synagogue, since expediency and personal safety were considerations that did not influence him. But he proclaimed nothing else. He needed to have his discovery clear in his own mind before he taught anyone else, and no one could help him in this. He went off alone into Arabia "instead of consulting with any human being or going up to Jerusalem" to see the apostles. (Galatians 1:16–17)

Paul habitually fought his battles in his own way, alone, in the same spirit of independence that in his young manhood had made him secretly restless under the domination of the Jewish Law. He stayed in Arabia until he was sure that he was at least on the right road and then went back to Damascus to appall the brotherhood and endanger his own life by proclaiming the doctrine he had worked out for himself. Paul did not go to see Peter in Jerusalem until three years later, and even then it was as a mark of respect to one of the leaders of the church rather than from any desire to be instructed.

Peter, meanwhile, had been fighting a private battle of his own in connection with the same Law that had once dominated Paul.

Peter was a good Jew and he naturally strove to obey the dictates of the Law, instructing his followers to do the same. It never occurred to him that the message he preached was intended for anyone but a Jew or a convert to Judaism, since it was to the Jews alone that the Messiah had been promised. If any Gentile wished to acknowledge the Messiah, he had to enter in through the door of Judaism to be accepted, and every convert was expected to obey the Jewish Law in all its particulars.

The first break in the armor of Peter's orthodoxy had been unwittingly made by Saul. His persecution scattered the brotherhood and forced Philip, one of the apostles, to go to Samaria. Philip preached so successfully in that despised city that Peter went down to confirm the work he had done, and although the Samaritans were the traditional enemies of the Jews they received his message so eagerly that Peter became a little less sure of the value of his own orthodoxy.

Peter's uncertainty was increased by a vision that came to him one day as he was standing on a rooftop in Joppa waiting for his dinner. He saw a multitude of birds and animals spread before him and heard a voice telling him to eat. Peter answered, "I have never eaten anything that was not ceremonially cleansed." (Acts 10:14) It was the answer of a good Jew, and for it he received a direct reproof: "Do not call what God has cleansed unclean." (Acts 10:15)

Peter understood the reason for his vision when he received an invitation from the captain of an Italian regiment to visit him. Peter went at once, breaking the rigid law that a Jew might not associate with a foreigner in the latter's house: "God has taught me not to call anyone vulgar or unclean." (Acts 10:28) Peter deeply shocked the conservative element in his own party by what he had done, and it took all his authority to convince them that "God shows no partiality but welcomes the man of any nation who reveres him and does what is right." (Acts 10:34–35) The anxious conservatives might have found the same view expressed in their own Scriptures if they had looked.

It was extremely difficult for any orthodox man to accept the idea that a Gentile might become a Christian without first being converted to Judaism. The only man who accepted it at once and without any reservations was Paul, the former Pharisee, and Luke says that the rest were "all afraid of him, for they could not believe that he was really a disciple." (Acts 9:26) The courageous work he had done in Damascus and the support of a prominent church member named Barnabas finally made Paul acceptable in Jerusalem, but he made so many enemies there that the church was obliged for its own sake to send him back to Tarsus. Barnabas came to him there with the news that a group of Gentiles at Antioch were trying to follow the new way and needed instruction, and the two men went to Antioch together and established a church among the Greeks. It was at Antioch that they were first given the name of Christians, from the Greek word for Messiah.

From this point onward the center of interest in Luke's Book of Acts shifts from Peter to Paul. Peter was the head of the well-established church in Judea, but Paul dreamed of bringing his message to the whole of the known world. This work was hardly begun and if it was ever to be accomplished there could be no line drawn between the Gentile and the Jew. Paul had been a Pharisee, trained in the rigid separatism of the Law, yet he was the only active Christian leader who knew that a policy of exclusion would be self-defeating.

Paul had a lively quarrel with Peter on this subject. Peter had been doing his best, slowly and painfully, to free himself from his inherited faith in an exclusive religion, and he was still not quite sure that he was doing the proper thing. Nor was he the only church leader in the movement. James and John were also "regarded as pillars of the church" (Galatians 2:9), and while John was characteristically silent on the whole question, James had very decided views about it. James was an extremely devout Jew and his rigid adherence to the letter of the Law had its effect on Peter. As Paul remarked bluntly, "Until some people came from James he used to eat with the heathen, but after they came he began to draw back and hold aloof, for fear of the party of circumcision." (Galatians 2:12) So great was Peter's influence that even the liberal Barnabas followed his example. But Paul refused to, and he lectured Peter to his face in public for allowing himself to be misled.

Neither Peter nor James bore Paul any ill will for his candor. On the contrary, they made every effort to understand his point of view. Matters were finally brought to a head over the question of circumcision, the conservative members of the church insisting that every Gentile had to be circumcised in order to become a Christian. A formal meeting was called in Jerusalem and both sides presented their arguments with some heat. The meeting was threatening to get out of order when Peter rose and quieted the tumult.

Peter reminded the embattled conservatives that he was their leader and yet he had been the first to bring the message to the Gentiles. He said also that the complicated Jewish Law had never been successfully followed in all its details by anyone, "a yoke that neither our forefathers nor we have been able to bear." (Acts 15:10) Then James, the orthodox, got up and supported Peter. "We ought not to put obstacles in the way of those of the heathen who are turning to God." (Acts 15:19) The influence of the two men swung the meeting in Paul's favor against the "party of circumcision," and Paul was free to make Gentiles into Christians without making them Jews first.

Paul's struggles as a missionary are recorded in the Book of Acts, but Paul's own letters give a hint of an inward, more personal and more difficult struggle. He faced misunderstandings with the Mother Church in Jerusalem; he faced lack of funds, disloyalty and constant physical danger from mobs, Roman officials, and the outraged supporters of orthodox Judaism. But above all he faced the difficulty of imparting to anyone the vision he had seen on the road to Damascus, the vision that had changed his life and set his feet on the road to freedom.

Paul found it almost impossible to fire his converts with his own blazing sense of conviction, the conviction that upheld him through shipwreck and prison and the constant threat of death. They were all willing to accept Jesus as a Messiah who had never died and was coming back to judge the world, and they were even willing to live lives of hopeful virtue in preparation for his coming; but most of them refused to go any farther. They anxiously asked Paul whether women should wear veils in church, how men should manage the question of divorce and whether it was wrong to eat meat that had been offered to idols; they argued at great length about the merits of their respective teachers. But none of them asked the way to find God.

Some of the converts even decided to be on the safe side and accept both circumcision under the old law and baptism under the new, so that whichever side was right they could be assured of salvation; and one of Paul's sternest letters arose from this well-intentioned precaution on the part of the people of Galatia. Paul was not preaching a new creed. He was preaching a way of life, one that had to be lived to be understood. It was not a formula that could be subscribed to without any further responsibility, but this was a point that almost none of his followers seemed to understand.

The story of Paul as given in the Acts is the history of his struggle with Roman authority, Jewish orthodoxy and mob prejudice. The story of Paul as given in his letters is the equally courageous but more heartbreaking struggle with his own churches. He wrestled with the inevitable growth of factions, the squabbles over precedence, the introducing of "divisions and difficulties" and arguments over food and drink—questions that troubled his converts so much that Paul had to fill pages answering them instead of dealing with the "new creation." (Galatians 6:15)

Paul told them to "act like men" (1 Cor. 16:13) but they persisted in acting like children. And it was like children, "babies in Christian living," (1 Cor. 3:1) that Paul treated them. It was not because they were worthy of it that he poured out to them all the splendor of his intellect and the fervor of his faith. As he said once, "God loves a man who is glad to give." (2 Cor. 9:7) And Paul was glad to lavish everything he had on his churches, even though little of it was ever accepted.

Paul faced both physical and mental torment to build his churches. "Five times I have been given one less than forty lashes by the Jews. I have been beaten three times by the Romans, I have been stoned once, I have been shipwrecked three times, a night and a day I have been adrift at sea; with my frequent journeys, in danger from rivers, danger from robbers, danger from my own people, danger from the heathen, danger in the city, danger in the desert, danger at sea, danger from false brothers, through toil and hardship, through many a sleepless night, through hunger and thirst, often without food and exposed to cold. And besides everything else, the thing that burdens me every day is my anxiety about all the churches." (2 Cor. 11:24–28) Paul had no wish to boast of what he had endured, but the people of Corinth made it necessary when they began to doubt his right to be an apostle at all. "I have been making a fool of myself, but you forced me to do it." (2 Cor. 12:11) Otherwise he seldom spoke of his difficulties or the heavy burden of anxiety he carried over the welfare of his churches.

If Paul had cared only for the letter of his gospel rather than for the spirit of it he might have been well content, for he left a trail of flourishing churches behind him. He followed the great trade routes that the Romans guarded and kept open, and his talent for organization made him quick to use every advantage that the civilization of Rome gave him. In his long years of missionary work, even before he went abroad, he had developed to a superlative degree his sympathetic understanding of other points of view, so that he could speak to Jews as a Jew and to Greeks as a Greek without altering in any way the essential facts of his message. In the cities he visited he found it an advantage to speak in the Jewish synagogues, which democratically welcomed any Jew as guest speaker if he knew his Scriptures and which attracted a large number of non-Jews by the dignity and simplicity of the services. Paul had, moreover, the protection of his Roman citizenship and availed himself of it to the fullest extent.

As a result of these things, and above all of his tireless endeavor, Paul created the beginnings of a large organization in the Roman provinces and even dreamed of carrying his gospel to great Rome itself. But no one knew better than he that the number of churches he founded was no guarantee in itself of the success of his mission; what mattered was the individual, how successfully he had found the way of life and how honestly he was walking in it. It was for the individual that Paul strove.

Meanwhile the enemies against him accumulated. He was even unpopular with some of the Jewish Christians in Jerusalem, who did not think he was sufficiently zealous in upholding the Law. When he returned to Jerusalem to report on his work among the Gentiles, his friends did what they could to convince the city that Paul was still a devout Jew. On their advice he went through the purification rites to reassure the "zealous upholders of the Law" (Acts 21:20) but the estrangement between the two points of view was too deep. The orthodox Jews started a riot against him, claiming that he had desecrated the temple by bringing a Gentile into it, and they dragged him into the street and nearly succeeded in killing him. Paul's death was prevented only by the prompt arrival of a Roman regiment to quell the riot.

The Roman officer had no idea what to do with his prisoner. He brought him before the Sanhedrin to find out what charge the Jews were bringing against him, but the Sanhedrin allowed itself to be ruled by emotion rather than reason and the meeting ended in an uproar. Forty Jews took an oath to kill Paul, and for the prisoner's own protection he was sent north to the governor at Caesarea.

Finally Paul arrived in the Rome he had dreamed of, in chains and still hounded by the implacable enmity of a small group of excited upholders of the Law. Once there, however, he was no longer treated as a prisoner except that a soldier was commissioned to guard him. Paul was allowed to live in rented lodgings and to preach freely, with no greater hindrance than that which his listeners gave him by failing to understand what he was trying to teach. Mostly Jews, they visited him in large numbers, willing to give the new sect a hearing but wholly unable to agree with it; and the Acts of the Apostles ends with the beginning of a complete separation between Judaism and Christianity. "Understand then that this message of God's salvation has been sent to the heathen. They will listen to it." (Acts 28:28)

Yet it was not only among the Jews that Paul encountered the people who are "ready to learn but never able to comprehend the truth." (2 Timothy 3:7) He met them everywhere, and if he was the one upon whom the burden of their failure fell most heavily it was because no other worker in the field made so many converts. Paul had a very high standard of what a Christian should be, and there were probably not a dozen men in all his churches who lived up to it. In fact, it was only Paul who could really have followed Paul's Christianity, since it was only Paul who had seen the vision on the road to Damascus. He tried patiently to transmit the vision to others, but very seldom did he succeed in striking the spark which meant that another man had caught the reflection of his own vision and was setting out to find God for himself.

The early Christian church in Jerusalem was a little group of men and women who met in an upstairs room to thank God for having known Jesus. They had all seen Jesus alive again after the crucifixion, and in the glory of that knowledge there was no room for anything else. They were of "one mind."

All this changed when they went out into the world to tell the people that the Messiah had come. They began at once to experience difficulties, and the difficulties multiplied in direct ratio to the number of converts that were brought into the church. By the very terms of the faith they taught they were obliged to bring their message to everyone—Jews and Gentiles, governors and slaves, mystics and theologians, honest seekers after truth and wealthy old ladies who wanted an interesting new religion to while away the time; and no two people received the message in the same way.

The very fact that the message offered freedom was in itself a difficulty, especially since it was a freedom that rejected the safeguards of the old Jewish Law. There were always people who would announce, "We are without any sin," (1 John 1:8) without attempting to prove it. There were always people who became absorbed in what they felt to be the esoteric side of the new religion, forgetting that it was intended to be practical. There were people who took their new faith too hard, "men with seared consciences who forbid people to marry and insist on abstinence from certain kinds of food that God created." (1 Timothy 4:3) There were the theologically minded, with a "morbid craving for speculations and arguments." (1 Timothy 6:4) Above all, there was the average, easy-going man who adopted the new religion because it gave him comfort and then went on living the way he had before, content to wait for a future kingdom to be established by the Messiah on earth and having no conception of what Paul meant by the great race that was to be run, the ceaseless striving that Paul himself had entered into to find the kingdom.

The apostles did their best to transmit their own vision to the people. But they could not do it, any more than Jesus had been able to transmit to his disciples his own understanding of God. Not even Jesus could give a man the truth unless he was capable of accepting it.

The apostles did their best, and their best was excellent. But they found more and more that they were obliged to organize and exhort and warn and threaten and punish where they had expected only to teach. No one knew better than they that the truth could not be organized, but there was nothing else they could do. The Church was no longer of "one mind."

THE LETTERS OF PAUL

I have worked harder than any of them.

1 Corinthians 15:10

There is no record of the convictions of the men who founded the Christian church except through their letters; and the majority of these are Paul's, since he did more traveling than any of the other apostles. The series of churches he established in Europe and Asia made letter-writing a necessity if he wanted to keep in touch with them, and his congregations saw Paul so seldom that they preserved whatever he wrote with reverent care.

Since Paul was the only early Christian to leave in writing a moderately full account of his views, it was from Paul that most of the tenets of a later Christianity were derived. It is not particularly easy to build up a theology from Paul's letters, since they were written at such a variety of times to such a variety of people that they frequently contradict each other. It is merely easier to do it with Paul's letters than with any of the others.

As a result, Paul is too often read in the light of a later theology, his most local and contemporary remarks translated into eternal verities. This would not have pleased Paul himself. He had very little respect for tradition and pained even the conservatives of his own day by the insistence with which he demanded individual freedom and individual responsibility in religion.

To read Paul fairly, it is necessary to remember two things. The first, and most obvious, is that his letters were letters, not essays or formal tracts. Most of Paul's teaching was done by word of mouth.

The second point, and it is one that is frequently forgotten, is that the man who wrote the letters was by birth and training a

15

Pharisee. As he himself says, "I surpassed many of my own age among my people in my devotion to Judaism, I was so fanatically devoted to what my forefathers had handed down." (Galatians 1:14) Paul left the sect when he became a Christian because he deliberately forsook its basic principle: the Law. But there were other principles he did not forsake, and it did not occur to him it was possible to forsake them.

It is important to remember, in the case of Paul as in that of the other apostles, that they were Jews before they became Christians and that a large part of their creed which is supposed to be the contribution of Christianity is actually Jewish. The idea of the immortality of the soul, of heaven and hell, angels, demons, Satan as the prince of evil spirits, the New Jerusalem as the home of the blessed, resurrection of the dead, eternal punishment of sinners, the Messiah as the "Son of Man" who was to judge the earth—all these were orthodox Jewish doctrines in the first century and the apostles believed them as Jews, not as Christians. Especially was this true of Paul, since it was the Pharisees who had been largely responsible for promulgating these doctrines, and Paul had been brought up as a Pharisee of the strictest kind.[1]

The Jewish religion offered two ways of seeking God as represented in two parallel religious institutions, the synagogue and the temple. The synagogue offered a way of reconciliation to God through personal righteousness; the temple offered a way of reconciliation through sacrifice. Both ways were very ancient and both were followed reverently by every good Jew.

The synagogue taught that the way to find God was through righteousness. This righteousness, however, was not based on any individual standard of virtue. Its basis was the Law, the holy Law that had been given by God to Moses and had been decreed in heaven as the property of the Jewish race before the world began.

---

[1] See *The Search For God,* for a fuller discussion of the doctrines of the Pharisees.

This was the written Law. There was also the oral Law, equally holy but rather less ancient, whose function it was to interpret the written Law of Moses and make it applicable to everyday living. If a Jew followed these two aspects of the Law faithfully he might safely expect eternal salvation. The Law was extremely difficult to follow in all its details, but the majority of Jews were only too glad to have their future mapped out for them and gloried in the difficulties as a rocky road that led to God and eternal bliss.

The way of the temple was the even older way of sacrifice, glorified by all the emotional ecstasy that marble halls and incense and great music could give it. The shedding of innocent blood as expiation for sin is probably the oldest religious idea in the world, and this was the fundamental theory behind every lamb and bullock and turtle dove that found its way to the high altars and death. Every offering had to be perfect, without blemish of any kind, and with it the soul that had sinned became reconciled to God. The climax came on the great Day of Atonement when the high priest, robed and crowned and in all his glory of gold and jewels, entered alone into the innermost sanctuary and there offered in silence a sacrifice for the nation, a sin-offering made by one man for all the people.

These two ideas of reconciliation were both based on the doctrine that sin came into the world through Adam and was shared by all his sons. They had belonged to Paul's race since the earliest times and were as familiar to him as the air he breathed.

Like all Jews, Paul was dominated by the idea of sin; but, unlike most Jews, he was not satisfied by the two ways of release that were offered through Judaism. He was not sufficiently emotional to be moved by the beauty of the temple services and to be exalted by that beauty into a sense of union with God; and he was too intelligent to shut his eyes to the underlying weakness of the Law. For the Law could not help a man to be good. It could only punish him if he failed, and so harshly that if he broke a Sabbath ordinance for the third time he was liable to death by stoning. The Law did not help a man to free himself from the sense of sin; it only defined the sin, as Paul himself had discovered. "If it had not been for the Law, I should never have learned what sin was; I should not have known what it was to covet if the Law had not said, 'You must not covet.' That command gave sin an opening . . . for sin is lifeless without law." (Romans 7:7–8) Adam was an example of the failure of the first "Thou shalt not" and Paul found that the system worked no better in his own day.

When Paul experienced his vision on the road to Damascus, it had its most immediate effect on this struggle of his with the Law. Paul was never willing to describe his vision, since there are "things that must not be told, which no human being can repeat." (2 Cor. 12:4) But there can be no doubt of its general impression upon him. Paul's vision of Jesus offered him what Jesus had always offered: freedom. And to Paul this meant freedom from the Law, since it was to the Law that he was most heavily in bondage.

When Paul became a Christian, he did not preach that the Law had been set aside. "The Law itself is holy, and each command is holy, just and good." (Romans 7:12) But the Law had been fulfilled. Its aim was righteousness, and by union with the Christ a new way of righteousness had been offered, one that did not punish the sinner but instead destroyed the sin. The Law of Moses no longer had any force with true Christians, because they had lost the sense of sin that was the only reason for the existence of the Law. "The Law no longer applies to us; for we have died to what once controlled us, so that we can now serve in the new spirit, not under the old letter." (Romans 7:6)

From that time forward, Paul called his old conception of religion "the religion of death." (2 Cor. 3:7) Its law was based on condemnation and "there is no condemnation any more for those who are in union with Christ Jesus." (Romans 8:1) The new law was the law of freedom, "not a consciousness of servitude that has been imparted to you, to fill you with fear again, but the consciousness of adoption as sons." (Romans 8:15) "You are no longer a slave, but a son; and if a son, then an heir, made so by God." (Galatians 4:7)

It was this conviction of freedom from the Law that alienated Paul from his fellow-Christians who insisted on remaining orthodox Jews. The Law taught, and every good Jew believed, that certain kinds of food were unclean and could not be eaten. Paul said: "Nothing is unclean in itself; a thing is unclean only to the man who regards it as unclean." (Romans 14:14) Every Jew was taught the profound significance of circumcision, the rite that had been sacred since Abraham. Paul said: "Being circumcised or being uncircumcised does not make any difference; all that matters is keeping God's commands." (1 Cor. 7:19) Deep-rooted in the Jewish heart was the unutterable sanctity of the Sabbath. Paul said: "One man thinks one day better than another, while another thinks them all alike. Everybody must be fully convinced in his own mind." (Romans 14:5)

The only rule he laid down was that each man should strive honestly to live up to his own standards, whatever they might be. "Keep the faith you have to yourself, as between God and you . . . The man who has misgivings about eating and then eats is thereby condemned, for he is not following his convictions and anything that does not rest on conviction is wrong." (Romans 14:22–23) Paul had a lack of respect for the minutiae of religion remarkable in any man, but almost incredible in anyone who had been a rigid Pharisee and "fanatically devoted" to the Jewish Law. From this much the vision he had seen on the road to Damascus had completely released him and he felt only compassion for the men who were still in bondage. "I can testify to their sincere devotion to God, but it is not an intelligent devotion." (Romans 10:2)

Yet if Paul found himself freed from the Jewish Law, in many other respects he remained a son of Judaism. The dominant idea of sin, the sin that came through Adam, was still strong in him, and equally strong was the temple idea of the power of sacrifice, the shedding of innocent blood to reconcile God and his sinning creation. Paul had no wish to free himself from this, for in it Paul and his fellow-Christians found an explanation for the base indignity of Jesus' crucifixion.

The Jewish apocalypses all taught that when the Messiah came he would come in glory, destroying the world, judging the sinners and lifting the righteous into heaven. All the brotherhood, from Paul down, believed that this was still going to happen and waited hopefully for Jesus to come back and fulfill his mission. But the doctrine of the Second Coming still did not explain why God should have allowed his messenger to be executed on a cross, instead of making him the great ruler that had been promised.

The answer the apostles found for this was purely Jewish; it was the temple idea of a single sin-offering for the people. Jesus was the high priest who offered alone an atonement for the sins of the people, except that the sacrifice he offered was not a spotless lamb but his own body. In the same way that the sacrifice of the high priest on the Day of Atonement reconciled all Jews to God, the sacrifice of Jesus on the cross reconciled all men to God if they would believe in him as the Messiah. "God showed him publicly dying as a sacrifice of reconciliation to be taken advantage of through faith." (Romans 3:25) Through this sacrifice men could find union with God, Who had been alienated by their sins, and they would be able to enter the kingdom that the Messiah would establish when he came again. It was to offer this opportunity that the Messiah had made his first appearance, since through it he was able "to reconcile to God all things on earth or in heaven, making this peace through his blood shed on the cross." (Colossians 1:20)

Since Paul was a Jew he had no difficulty in accepting this explanation of the crucifixion; but he added to it something of his own. He saw in the death of Jesus on the cross a death to sin and an awakening to a new life, so that everyone who believed in him and achieved union with him would be able to do in his moral nature what Jesus had done in the physical. "When he died, he became once for all dead to sin; the life he now lives is a life in relation to God. So you also must think of yourselves as dead to sin but alive to God, through union with Christ Jesus." (Romans 6:10–11)

Paul continually used the crucifixion as a symbol of a new birth, the door into a new life. "Through baptism we have been buried with him in death, so that just as he was raised from the dead through the Father's glory, we too may live a new life . . . Our old self was crucified with him, to do away with our sinful body, so that we might not be enslaved to sin any longer." (Romans 6:4–6) Paul did not apologize for the crucifixion. He gloried in it and made it the basis of his teaching. "I never want to boast of anything but the cross of our Lord Jesus Christ, on which the world has been crucified to me and I have been to the world." (Galatians 6:14)

In general, Paul's attitude towards the Messiah was that of any orthodox Jew. The writers of the various Jewish apocalypses, and especially the author of the influential Book of Enoch, had established firmly in the minds of the Jewish people the kind of Christ that was going to appear on the great Day of the Lord. He was "the Righteous One," the "Elect One," the "Son of Man." He had been chosen for his great office before the creation of the world. "Yea, before the sun and the signs were created, before the stars of the heavens were made, his name was named before the Lord." He was to be a "light to the Gentiles, and a hope to those who are troubled of heart" and it was in him that the righteous should find immortal life. "For in his name they are saved." On his arrival the forces of evil would be conquered and the dead raised. Sinners would be plunged into the jaws of hell while the righteous would be clothed "with garments of glory" and walk in the "light of eternal life." "For I and my Son will be united with them forever."

The Book of Enoch, from which these quotations were taken, was widely read by the early Christians. It is directly quoted in the Book of Jude (Jude 1:14) and its teachings are echoed in the letters of nearly all the apostles. The book itself was believed to be very old and its description of the day of judgment was accepted with unquestioning reverence.

The early Christian Church believed on this and similar authority that the Last Day was imminent, and Paul, like everyone else, was sure that the time was near "when our Lord Jesus appears from heaven with his mighty angels in a blaze of fire and takes vengeance on the godless." (2 Thess. 1:7–8) Some of the churches began to grow disturbed because their members were dying and would not be there to welcome the Day of the Lord, but Paul comforted them with the assurance that the dead equally with the living would share in the glory of the new Day that the Christ would bring. "For the Lord himself, at the summons, when the archangel calls and God's trumpet sounds, will come down from heaven, and first those who died in union with Christ will rise; then those of us who are still living will be caught up with them on clouds into the air to meet the Lord." (1 Thess. 4:16–17)

Yet Paul did not always think of Jesus as the Messiah of Jewish tradition. He had himself seen him on the road to Damascus, and for the advent of this Christ there was nothing in Judaism to prepare him. The Christ of Paul's own experience was not a conquering judge. He was "the eldest of many brothers." (Romans 8:29) While he was truly the son of God, this was not a private privilege that belonged to him alone. "For all who are guided by God's spirit are God's sons." (Romans 8:14) Jesus was the "likeness of God" (2 Cor. 4:4) but any man could learn to claim the same likeness. "For you have stripped off your old self with its ways and have put on that new self newly made in the likeness of its Creator, to know him fully." (Colossians 3:10) To know God fully was not something that was going to occur with a last trump on the Day of Judgment. It was instead a gradual illumination that began as soon as any man accepted the way of release that Jesus offered, as soon as he "died with Christ to material ways of looking at things." (Colossians 2:20) Jesus had taken away the veil which, in the symbolism of the temple, hid all men from the secret place of God and he had therefore made it possible for all men to be re-created as God's sons, to know him fully. "Wherever the spirit of the Lord is, there is freedom. And all of us, reflecting the splendor of the Lord in our unveiled faces, are being changed into likeness to him, from one degree of splendor to another." (2 Cor. 3:17–18) Paul did not learn this from any Jewish doctrine. He learned it from having seen Jesus, the one man who possessed perfect freedom, face to face.

Paul had not known Jesus during his ministry. Therefore he assumed that this freedom had belonged to Jesus before his birth and was reassumed after the crucifixion, having been deliberately laid aside in the interim. According to Paul's view it was not until after the resurrection that Jesus had again lived "a life in relation to God." (Romans 6:10) This was a misunderstanding which only John, of all the apostles, did not share. The rest of them felt that eternal life was something to be achieved after death, an assumption that was contrary to what Jesus himself taught but a natural one for any Jew.

Paul expressed the orthodox Jewish faith in immortality very nobly more than once. "The body is sown in decay, it is raised free from decay . . . It is sown in weakness, it is raised in strength. It is a physical body that is sown, it is a spiritual body that is raised." (1 Cor. 15: 42–44) "I know that if this earthly tent that I live in is taken down, God will provide me a building in heaven to live in, not built by human hands but eternal." (2 Cor. 5:1) Yet even Paul rebelled against the necessity of dying. "I who am still in my tent sigh with anxiety, because I do not want to be stripped of it but to put on the other over it." (2 Cor. 5:4) It did not occur to Paul that Jesus had accepted the crucifixion to prove that in his relationship to God there was no room for weakness or decay and that this fact nullified the whole idea of death. Paul was a Jew and he had been brought up to believe that only through death could eternal life be found.

Paul tried to put the new wine that Jesus offered him into the old wineskins of orthodox Judaism, and the effort naturally involved him in inconsistencies. The existence that Jesus called the kingdom of heaven and that Paul called "the glorious freedom of the children of God" (Romans 8:21) was obviously a spiritual condition to Paul and yet he expected it to come as the result of a physical Day of Judgment. It was to come in the future, accompanied by the sound of trumpets, and yet Paul knew that it also belonged to the present. "If anyone is in union with Christ he is a new being; the old state of things has passed away." (2 Cor. 5:17) Paul referred more than once to a "new creation" (Galatians 6:15) that was of the present rather than of the future, and if he had not been so dominated by the Jewish idea of future salvation he might have been able to carry the implication of his own phrase to its logical conclusion.

But concerning the nature of this salvation Paul was clear enough. To anyone who found union with Christ, Paul offered a complete understanding of God, the ability to know God "as fully as God knows me." (1 Cor. 13:12) He offered a complete brotherhood. "There is no room for 'Jew' and 'Greek'; there is no room for 'slave' and 'freedman'; there is no room for 'male' and 'female;' for in union with Christ Jesus you are all one." (Galatians 3:28) He offered a release from the bondage of limitation, from the finity that Jesus had called "the world"; for "creation itself would be set free from its bondage to decay and have the glorious freedom of the children of God." (Romans 8:21) And, above all, he offered love.

Paul had a very clear sense of the love Jesus had shown in undergoing the crucifixion, even though he somewhat misunderstood its purpose, and he prayed that his churches might try to understand that love, "so far beyond our understanding." (Ephesians 3:19) In spite of Paul's arguments and his intricate rabbinic way of reasoning, the love which he recognized in Jesus was the basis of his own religion. It was this love that had cast out his own fear of the Law; and he trusted it as he trusted nothing else because he knew that it came from God. "I am convinced that neither death nor life nor angels nor their hierarchies nor the present nor the future nor any supernatural forces either of height or depth will be able to separate us from the love God has shown in Christ Jesus our Lord." (Romans 8:38–39)

To realize that love, it was necessary to love in return. One of Paul's letters to the people of Corinth, an attempt to render decisions in certain matters of church discipline, suddenly drops the whole question in the middle, states abruptly, "I will show you a far better way," (1 Cor. 13:1) and gives instead Paul's own creed as a Christian. "If I can speak with the tongues of men and even of angels, but have no love, I am only a noisy gong or a clashing cymbal. If I am inspired to preach and know all the secret truths and possess all knowledge, and if I have such perfect faith that I can move mountains, but have no love, I am nothing. Even if I give away everything I own and give myself up, but do it in pride, not love, it does me no good . . . Love will never die out. If there is ecstatic speaking, it will cease. If there is knowledge, it will pass away. For our knowledge is imperfect and our preaching is imperfect. But when perfection comes, what is imperfect will pass away. When I was a child, I talked like a child, I thought like a child, I reasoned like a child. When I became a man, I put aside my childish ways. For now we are looking at a dim reflection in a mirror, but then we shall see face to face. Now my knowledge is imperfect, but then I shall know as fully as God knows me." (1 Cor. 13:1–12)

Paul was a great man. He knew that what he taught was not the whole truth as Jesus had known it, that his knowledge was imperfect as his preaching was imperfect and that both of them would pass away. But he knew that his love was reality and that, when all the half-truths had vanished and he saw God face to face, the love would still endure. For the rest, he was still a child peering into a darkened mirror. It was only Jesus who had become an adult and Paul strove to reach the same condition, "mature manhood and that full measure of development found in Christ." (Ephesians 4:13) He never tried to make his converts believe he had attained full knowledge, any more than they. "Brothers, I do not consider that I have captured it yet, only, forgetting what is behind me and straining toward what lies ahead, I am pressing toward the goal, for the prize to which God through Christ Jesus calls us upward." (Philippians 3:13–14)

Paul knew what his goal was, and he had the love and the whole-hearted desire for truth which made it inevitable he would eventually reach it. But he carried with him two heavy burdens, and they weighed him down more than was needful in the race he was running. The first was his training in Jewish theology and the second was his complete devotion to his churches.

His churches were undoubtedly a drag on Paul. They took everything he had to give—his time, his labor and his thought—and even the best of them gave him little in return. In order to raise them to his level he was obliged to sink first to theirs, and he stayed there, as the letters show, almost continually. Corinth was the best of the cities and called forth the most beautiful of the letters, yet even to the men of Corinth Paul wrote: "Brothers, I could not treat you as spiritual persons; I had to treat you . . . as babies in Christian living. I fed you with milk, not solid food, for you were not ready for it. Why, you are not ready for it now." (1 Cor. 3:1–3)

Paul had apparently pledged himself to write to his churches "only what you can read and understand" (2 Cor. 1:13) and it was very seldom that he wrote forgetting his audience. The first letter to the Corinthians contains such a passage, the great one on love, and it is heartbreaking to see Paul drop the subject that was so dear to his own heart to take up again, in a change of mood that is almost physically jarring, the old questions of church discipline. Paul the searcher did not care whether or not women kept their heads covered in church; but Paul the teacher cared, because the question was one that troubled the congregation, and anything that was important to the congregation was important to him.

Out of his love for the churches Paul tried to carry them with him in the race he was running, the race that each man must run alone. And out of his allegiance to the religion of his forefathers he tried also to carry with him a weight of tradition that could not be reconciled with the teaching that Jesus brought. But stronger than Paul the organizer or Paul the Pharisee was Paul the searcher, the son of Israel who had set out to find God for himself. And it was this Paul who knew that where he now saw God dimly, as in a reflection in a mirror, he would see him eventually face to face.

THE REST OF THE LETTERS

One a hundred, and another sixty, and another thirtyfold.

Matthew 13:23

Very little of the correspondence of the early church was saved. With the exception of Paul's letters there are only eight in existence: one from James, one from Jude, two attributed to Peter, three to John, and a letter or essay which was later given the title of Letter to the Hebrews. Two of John's are so short that they can hardly be called more than notes, and Peter's second letter is not generally believed to be authentic.

This leaves five letters on which to base a judgment of five men, and it is well to remember that such a judgment can only be fragmentary. If Peter had no other testimony, no one could have guessed the quality of the ardent, impulsive disciple recorded in the gospels or the apostle who fought so gallantly against his own prejudices in the Acts.

The first of these eight letters, the Letter to the Hebrews, is anonymous. It was later attributed to various men, to Paul, to Barnabas, to Apollos and even to Luke, but there was never any real certainty in the early church as to its authorship. Clearly, however, it was written by a Jew, a man both brilliant and well-educated, and it is from its pronounced Judaism that the letter gets its name.

The Letter to the Hebrews is an attempt to explain and justify Christianity in terms of Judaism, to expound the new covenant of Jesus in the light of the old covenant of Moses. Its basic idea is that every aspect of the old religion was the shadow of a truth that had since been revealed in the new, and in developing this idea it shows even more clearly than Paul's letters the origin of the idea that Jesus sacrificed himself for the sins of the world.

27

The parallel, explicitly stated, is that of the great mediator, the Jewish high priest. Once every year he lifted the embroidered curtain that veiled the inner sanctuary of the temple and the unseen presence of God, and went inside alone to make an offering for the sins of all the people. This high priest had now been replaced by a greater one, who had thus become the only mediator between God and man. "But every high priest is appointed to offer gifts and sacrifices, and so this high priest also must have some sacrifice to offer." (Hebrews 8:3) This sacrifice was that of the crucifixion. "He went once for all, through that greater, more perfect tent of worship not made by human hands nor a part of our material creation, into the sanctuary, taking with him no blood of goats and calves, but his own, and secured our permanent deliverance." (Hebrews 9:11–12)

This is a purely Jewish argument and it comes from a religion whose basis was the theory that a reconciliation between God and man could only come through physical sacrifice. "In fact, under the Law, almost everything is purified with blood, and unless blood is poured out nothing is forgiven." (Hebrews 9:22)

It is, however, a very exalted kind of Judaism, having no formalism about it and asking only to find union with God. "Since then, brothers, we have free access to the sanctuary through the blood of Jesus, by the new, living way which he has opened for us ... and since we have in him a great priest set over the house of God, let us draw near to God in sincerity of heart and with perfect faith." (Hebrews 10:19–22) Jesus was the new way to God, the pathway of reconciliation which some of the older Jewish writers had called "wisdom" and to which they had attributed the creation of the world. "He is the reflection of God's glory, and the representation of his being, and bears up the universe by his mighty word." (Hebrews 1:3)

The author of Letter to the Hebrews was a Jew, writing to Jews and basing his whole argument on the tenets of orthodox Judaism. He was not, however, entirely a traditionalist, even though the force of his letter depends on tradition. His way of reading the Scriptures, for instance, was entirely his own. He saw the great men of his race not simply as holy prophets through whom God spoke his will, but as individuals struggling towards the light as he and his contemporaries were. They were sojourners in a strange land, striving to find a permanent country of their own. They had not discovered the whole truth; "they only saw it far ahead and welcomed the sight of it, recognizing that they themselves were only foreigners and strangers here on earth." (Hebrews 11:13) "It was little by little and in different ways that God spoke in old times to our forefathers through the prophets." (Hebrews 1:1) Yet this reasonable view of the limitations of the Old Testament did not prevent the author of the letter from choosing at random any text that might prove his point and then presenting it as an eternal verity. This was the way the texts were always used in the synagogues, and the author used the same method not necessarily because he believed in it himself but because his readers did.

In this he was very like Paul, who always tried to write on the level of his readers. Almost an echo of Paul, too, was his complaint, "I have much to say to you . . . but it is difficult to make it clear to you, because you have become so slow of apprehension." (Hebrews 5:11) Neither man got much assistance from his listeners in an effort to make them what Paul called "fellow-heirs" (Romans 8:17) and the author of Hebrews called "true partners with Christ." (Hebrews 3:14) Yet both men strove valiantly to offer "the new, living way" to the world and to follow it faithfully themselves. The success of either man cannot fairly be judged on the basis of letters alone, but there is no mistaking the reality of the desire itself, the desire that was leading them as it had led the men of the Old Testament "in search of a country of their own." (Hebrews 11:14)

The letter of James, the brother of Jesus, is of a different kind. James had a profound faith in the things that are seen and very little in the things that are unseen. It was this quality that made him unable to believe in his brother during the period of his ministry and then believe in him completely when Jesus offered the final proof of the resurrection. Since James had great faith in physical testimony he was naturally one of those who advocated circumcision, and it is easy to see why he failed to get on successfully with Paul, who taught that "what is seen is transitory but what is unseen is eternal." (2 Cor. 4:18) To James, the highest test of a good Christian was his morality, and he disapproved of what he felt to be Paul's failure to emphasize this point.

In spite of Paul's efforts to make himself clear he was continually being misunderstood. The writer of the Second Letter of Peter mentions the letters of "our dear brother Paul" and explains that "there are some things in them hard to understand, which ignorant, unsteadfast people twist to their own ruin." (2 Peter 3:16) This is an example of a difficulty so inherent in missionary work that even Paul, greatest of all missionaries, could not escape it. In spite of Paul's careful wording, there was no doubt that some of his students read into his teachings a glorification of a kind of mystical faith that could unite a man to God without any effort of his own so long as he "believed"; and it was as an antidote to this easygoing kind of Christianity that James wrote his letter.

There was never any danger that James could be misunderstood. He kept both feet firmly on the ground and dealt only with plain and simple matters that were well within the comprehension of any man. His letter deals only with Jewish morality and could equally well have been written if Jesus had never lived; but in a sense this is true of most of the apostles, who understood Jewish morality and Jewish theology much better than they understood Jesus. At least, what James knew he knew thoroughly, and his presentation of it has a straightforward honesty that is very attractive.

His letter makes no attempt to belittle the quality of faith. Anyone who asks God for wisdom "must ask with faith and without any doubt" (James 1:6) and such faith is of the utmost importance. The faith that James objects to is the shallow variety which has only an emotional reason for its existence and which can show no results. "If some brother or sister has no clothes and has not food enough for a day, and one of you says to them, 'Goodbye, keep warm and have plenty to eat,' without giving them the necessaries of life, what good does it do? So faith by itself, if it has no good deeds to show, is dead." (James 2:15–17) To prove the necessity of good deeds James quotes the example of Abraham's sacrifice of his son, (James 2:21) the same illustration that the author of Letter to the Hebrews used to prove the paramount necessity of faith only. (Hebrews 11:17) One of the great advantages of the Jewish system of quoting from single texts was that the same passage could be used to prove entirely opposite points of view, and frequently was.

While the general tone of James' letter is utilitarian, there are occasional flashes of something better. "No one should think when he is tempted that his temptation comes from God, for God is incapable of being tempted by evil, and he does not tempt anyone . . . Every good gift and every perfect gift is from heaven, and comes down from the Father . . . Of his own accord he brought us into being through the message of truth." (James 1:13–18) And James was capable of giving as good advice as any man ever gave: "Obey the message; do not merely listen to it and deceive yourselves. For anyone who merely listens to the message without obeying it is like a man who looks in a mirror at the face that nature gave him, and then goes off and immediately forgets what he looked like. But whoever looks at the faultless law that makes men free and keeps looking, so that he does not just listen and forget, but obeys and acts upon it, will be blessed." (James 1:23–25)

Peter's letter is again different. It does not show the very human man who appears in the gospels and the Acts of the Apostles. It shows only the chief of the elders and the acknowledged head of the church in Jerusalem, bending down to reassure a little congregation that had been scattered over Asia and threatened with persecution. It is a "short letter to encourage you" (1 Peter 5:12) and for the most part could have been written by any of the church elders.

The one thing that marks it as characteristic of Peter is its intensity, its strong sense of excitement. Peter does not ask his followers to bear their burdens with quiet patience; he asks them to "rejoice with triumphant, unutterable joy" (1 Peter 1:8)—not to endure only but to be unspeakably happy to endure. Peter does not ask his followers merely to believe in Jesus: "You must love him, though you have not seen him." (1 Peter 1:8) He does not ask them to treat each other with fairness and self-control: "You must love one another intensely." (1 Peter 1:22) And as for the threat of persecution, "Be glad that you are in a measure sharing the sufferings of the Christ, so that when his glory is revealed you may be triumphantly happy." (1 Peter 4:13)

This emphasis on a joyful endurance was to a certain extent characteristic of the whole early church. It was almost a necessity with the early Christians that they should believe in a future day of salvation that would compensate them for the cruelty with which they were being persecuted, and if Jewish tradition had not taught the existence of such a day they might almost have been obliged to invent one for themselves. Such a doctrine had no relation to the man who taught, "The kingdom of God is within you," (Luke 17:21) but it helped the early church to withstand the brutality of its foes.

The whole emphasis of Peter's letter is on this Day of the Lord: "The end of all things is near." (1 Peter 4:7) In preparation for the Last Day all Christians must live faithfully and honorably, servants submissive to their masters, wives to their husbands, husbands to the state, and all together, united in a loving brotherhood, they must remember "the mercy that you are to experience when Jesus Christ is revealed." (1 Peter 1:13) Against this, the persecution that has been experienced will count for nothing. For "God, the giver of all mercy, who through your union with Christ has called you to his eternal glory, after you have suffered a little while will himself make you perfect, steadfast and strong." (1 Peter 5:10)

The second letter of Peter is sometimes attributed to a disciple of his, writing in the name of his master. The letter is primarily an attack upon teachers who attempt to circulate false doctrines and shake the people's faith in the imminent coming of the Messiah. And there is nothing, even in the Old Testament, more violent than the denunciations the author heaps on their unwitting heads. They "introduce destructive sects and deny the Master," (2 Peter 2:1) they defile the sacraments, they are greedy for the souls of others and try to lure them into immorality, and they try to make people disbelieve in the coming of the Day. But, says the author, in the very literary swing of the old prophets, "their condemnation has not been idle and their destruction has not slumbered." (2 Peter 2:3) The Day of the Lord will come suddenly, "the heavens will pass away with a roar, the heavenly bodies will burn up and be destroyed, and the earth and all its works will melt away." (2 Peter 3:10) Then will the evil men be dealt with as they deserve and fall to "swift destruction." (2 Peter 2:1)

It is not easy to believe that this was ever the doctrine of Peter, the disciple of Jesus, and the early church itself had doubts about the authority of the letter. Nevertheless, while the doctrine itself is the violently literal one of the Jewish apocalypses in its wholesale destruction of the world, this was a doctrine in which Peter believed and which was essentially the corollary of his faith that the good would be rewarded on the Last Day. If the good were to be rewarded, it was to be expected that the evil would be punished. Peter himself says of those that oppose the church that "they will have to answer for it to him who is ready to judge living and dead." (1 Peter 4:5) The second letter has its roots in this statement and is merely a detailed and violent expansion of it.

If Peter wrote this second letter it is obvious that he did it reluctantly. He was forced into the same position as Jude, another of the brothers of Jesus, who had intended to write on matters pertaining to the faith and found himself forced, like Peter, into a denunciation of evil men. "Dear friends, I was just on the point of writing you about our common salvation, when it became necessary to write and appeal to you to come to the defense of the faith . . . For some people have sneaked in among us—their doom was foretold long ago—godless persons who turn the mercy of our God into an excuse for immorality." (Jude 1:3–4) The letter continues with a denunciation quite as violent as that in the second letter of Peter and sometimes in almost the same wording. Those who defile the sacraments are like "leafless trees without fruit, doubly dead and uprooted; wild sea waves foaming up their own shame; wandering stars doomed forever to utter darkness." (Jude 1:12–13)

Jude did not like to denounce evil men; he would greatly have preferred to write about "our common salvation." Peter did not like to dwell on the necessity for endurance; he would much rather have told the glory of his own "triumphant, unutterable joy." Paul did not enjoy scolding his churches, or bending his vision of a perfect creation to their limited understanding; he would much rather have written of the glory of God. But the leaders of the church were obliged to write as they did, just as they were obliged to hold councils concerning the value of circumcision and the necessity of eating certain kinds of food.

These men were engaged in presenting a doctrine to the world, and unless they adapted it to the needs and to the understanding of the world it would never have been accepted. They were laboring to build a broad highway into the kingdom of heaven, and the more crowded the highway became the more difficulty the builders experienced in their efforts to keep it smooth and straight. The search for truth is an individual matter; it is difficult to make it a collective one. And it was in their valiant efforts to make it collective that the leaders of the early church had their hardest struggle and their least success.

Only one of the apostles did not spend his life laboring to build a strong church. This one was John, the disciple whom Jesus loved best. John could have been as prominent in the early church as Peter, yet he never availed himself of the position that would normally have been his. It was always Peter who made the speeches, even when John was with him. It was Peter who organized the congregations and led the councils. John did not even take sides when the question of circumcision came up, and as far as the records go he played no part whatever in any of the aspects of organization.

Only one important letter of John remains, and probably only one was written. He says in both his brief notes that he did not like to write letters and preferred to talk face to face. (2 John 1:12; 3 John 1:13) Yet if any proof were needed that John possessed none of the spirit that goes out to organize, this one letter is more than sufficient.

Paul's letters are those of a true missionary. He constantly considers the effect of his words on his readers, adapts his language to their intelligence, and gives exhaustive attention to various minor problems of church discipline in an effort to build wisely for the future. But John paid no attention to problems of church discipline and he never stopped to explain himself. He wrote in the steady light of his own spirit, almost wholly unmoved by the confusion around him, sure that anyone who really wanted the truth would find it and that it needed no compromise on John's part to aid the search.

John's idea of a church was a group of people who loved each other and who really wanted to find God. He knew well enough that the church as it was then constituted did not measure up to that ideal—that it contained people who fought to assume control, and people who wandered in a delighted haze of mysticism, and people who followed every new theory that was offered. He mentions in his letter the people who so misused the doctrine of freedom that they went around saying, "We are without any sin" without proving it (1 John 1:8) and he was well aware of the usual cliques and feuds that spring up whenever human beings are together. John knew all these things but he did not stop to concern himself with them. He was not writing a letter to point out the congregations' mistakes. He was writing it to offer them the truth, and if they were willing to accept the truth the mistakes would disappear. His primary object was not to analyze the shadows. It was to proclaim the light.

To accomplish this, John did something that no other writer in the New or the Old Testament ever did. He defined God. The prophets and the apostles had all attempted to explain the relationship of God to his worshiper. John went straight back to the source and began with God himself. "God is spirit." (John 4:24) "God is light." (1 John 1:5) "God is love." (1 John 4:8)

Nine words were enough for John's creed. He was rather like some mathematician who records on paper in a few deceptively simple combinations of letters and numbers the formula he has spent all his life finding, and who offers it without much comment since he knows it will be clear only to the individual who has spent his life in the same search.

Since God is light, any man who accepts God is the son of light. Since God is love, any man who accepts God knows the fullness of love. John saw no need, therefore, to counsel and exhort and warn. Jesus had brought the truth when he said, "God is light. There is no darkness in him at all," (1 John 1:5) and whoever acknowledged that truth would be free of his sins, his mistakes and of "everything wrong." (1 John 1:9) He would live as God's son, in union with him, even as Jesus himself had done.

In no other way could a man find the light than by claiming his identification with the God who was light itself. This was what John called "living the truth" (1 John 1:6) and in it could be found protection from the thing that frightened the early Christians most. "No one who is a child of God commits sin, for God's nature remains in his heart, and he cannot sin because he is a child of God." (1 John 3:9) Nor can he, for the same reason, know hatred; nor can he walk in darkness. "We live in the light just as he is in the light." (1 John 1:7)

John learned this way of working from Jesus, who taught that man was alive because God was *life,* and who proved it. Whether John proved it or not is unknown, but he had an almost intuitive understanding of the principle from which the proof could be derived.

The chief emphasis in John's letter is on love. Perhaps this was because so much of the early church had been founded on fear and "perfect love drives out fear." (1 John 4:18) To love was the one paramount obligation of the brotherhood, for "whoever does not love does not know God, since God is love." (1 John 4:8) This was the first great commandment to John, and the second was like it. "If anyone says, 'I love God,' and yet hates his brother, he is a liar; for whoever does not love his brother whom he has seen cannot love God whom he has not seen." (1 John 4:20) This is an echo of what Jesus himself said: "You must love the Lord your God with your whole heart, your whole soul and your whole mind. That is the great first command. There is a second like it: you must love your neighbor as you do yourself." (Matt. 22:37–39)

Love was not a kindly virtue with John, any more than it was with Jesus. Love was the basic necessity of living, and without it there could be no real life at all because without it God could never be found. "Anyone who does not love is still in death." (1 John 3:14)

John called Jesus the "message of life" (1 John 1:2) because he showed the way to know God, and "whoever obeys his message really has the love of God in perfection in his heart." (1 John 2:5) It was Jesus who loved his brothers so greatly that he laid down his life for their mistakes, and whoever follows him must have the same love in his heart. "Whoever says, 'I am always in union with him' must live just as he lived." (1 John 2:6) To live as Jesus lived means to love God, and "whoever continues to love keeps in union with God, and God with him." (1 John 4:16) For this a man may receive the hatred of the world, but "he who is in our hearts is greater than he who is in the world." (1 John 4:4)

John uses the term "world" to typify the hate that is in opposition to love, the darkness that is in opposition to light. In his gospel he used the term "Jews" to typify the same thing. John did not intend the words to be taken literally. He was himself a Jew and he certainly lived in the world. John used these terms as abbreviations for what he might otherwise have called the hatred felt by the darkness for the light that is going to cause its destruction.

The darkness itself John called the devil, and here again he was unlike his contemporaries. He never acknowledged the existence of any devils at all, apart from the one basic source of what he called "error." (1 John 4:6) He sometimes used phrases like "children of the world" and "children of the devil" and "anti-christs," but he meant the same thing that Jesus meant when he called Peter "Satan" (Matt. 16:23)—that is, the ignorance of the truth, which Peter happened to be expressing at the moment.

John also differed from his contemporaries in his expectations regarding the future. He had no intention of transferring what Paul called "the glorious freedom of the children of God" (Romans 8: 21) to any future Day of Judgment. The time was now and the place was within. He mentions the Day of Judgment once in his letter, but only to tell the churches there was no need to worry about it. "There is no fear in love, but perfect love drives out fear. For fear suggests punishment, and no one who feels fear has attained perfect love." (1 John 4:18) Since one of the fundamental reasons for the Day of Judgment was the idea of the necessity of punishment, John was really disposing of the whole conception of a Last Day.

To John, the destruction of "the world" was already taking place, not in a wild cataclysm of fire that would destroy the stars but by the steady pressure of the light that means understanding. Jesus had brought this light, the full understanding of God, and through it what John called the world was inevitably being destroyed. "The darkness is passing and the true light is already shining." (1 John 2:8)

There was no need to wait for a Last Day to discover the fatherhood of God. "Dear friends, we are God's children now." (1 John 3:2) As each man found this reality of sonship for himself he would be as Jesus was. "We shall be like him, for we shall see him as he is." (1 John 3:2) To make himself like Jesus was the one duty of a Christian, and it could be done only by understanding the reality that Jesus understood. "The son of God has come and has given us power to recognize him who is true." (1 John 5:20)

John wrote his letter for a specific reason, to show the followers of Jesus the way to eternal life. "I have written this so that you who believe in the son of God may know that you have eternal life." (1 John 5:13) He did not write it to instruct the churches, for "you do not need to have anyone teach you." (1 John 2:27) The only real teacher was the one that Jesus had left behind him, the "spirit of truth that comes from the Father" (John 15:26); and John knew that the greatest assistance that could be given the spirit of truth was to trust to its power completely.

All the apostles loved their churches and labored for them. Yet not even Paul showed such complete and such effective love as John did when he wrote, "You all know the truth. I do not write to you because you do not know it, but because you do know it and because no lie can come from the truth." (1 John 2:21) John was very well aware of the faults of the churches, but unlike the other apostles he did not believe that pointing them out would destroy them. Instead of taking up the sword against these mistakes John refused to acknowledge their existence, basing his refusal on the fact that God is light and that in his light there could be no darkness of misunderstanding.

This was John's way of praying for the churches, not to ask God for their safety but to know they were already safe. Jesus had said, "Whenever you pray or ask for anything, have faith that it has been granted you, and you shall have it." (Mark 11:24) And so John remained undisturbed, having faith that his prayer was already granted.

PART II

Note to The Reader

The Book of Revelation is carefully constructed, on an almost mathematical plan, as a single unit. It is assumed that the reader will treat it as such. It was not intended for casual reading.

It is assumed also that the reader is familiar with the final section, called "The Finding," of the author's *The Search for God*, and with the chapter called "Recapitulation" in *Science and Health With Key to the Scriptures* by Mary Baker Eddy.

The translation used is the King James Version, with an occasional variant reading. Quotations from other parts of the Bible are from the University of Chicago translation, to which I am indebted. I am indebted also to Richard Moulton for his comments in *The Modern Reader's Bible* on the structure of the book as a whole.

There is a glossary on page 97 of terms that are used frequently.

THE STRUCTURE
OF THE BOOK
OF REVELATION

Prologue

The Seven Visions
1. The receiving of the scroll.
2. The opening of the seven seals.
3. The sounding of the seven trumpets.
4. The birth of the man child; the appearance of the dragon and his deputies.
5. The seven vials of judgment; the destruction of Babylon.
6. Victory over the deputies of the dragon; the millennial kingdom; final destruction of the dragon.
7. The appearance of the holy city.

Epilogue

THE BOOK OF REVELATION

The highways are in their minds.

Psalms 84: 5

The Revelation of Saint John the Divine is written in a literary form which was very popular in its own day—that of the "apocalypse."

A great many of these apocalypses were produced in the first century. They were written to comfort the faithful in days of persecution and to promise them a Day of Judgment when the world would end in fire and smoke and a new world would be ushered in by God and his Messiah. The dead would be raised, the world judged and sinners plunged into torment, while the faithful would be rewarded by an eternity of bliss. Apocalypses of this kind were written by both Jews and Christians and were eagerly read.

Since the framework of the Book of Revelation is similar to that of these apocalypses, the majority of Biblical scholars have made an earnest effort to prove that the book is therefore just another manifestation of this contemporary belief in an imminent and literal end of the world.

Nevertheless, all attempts to interpret the Book of Revelation from this point of view have been a failure, and the more detailed and scholarly the attempt the greater the failure. One eminent New Testament scholar[1] wrote two thick volumes in an attempt to prove that the Book of Revelation was foretelling a literal Day of Judgment; but first he was obliged to omit everything in the book which did not

---

[1] R. H. Charles, *A Critical and Exegetical Commentary on the Revelation of St. John.* New York: Charles Scribner's Sons, 1920.

fit in with this theory and then he was obliged to rearrange the rest of it in a different order.

This is a risky thing to do with any book, but it is especially unwise to do it with the Book of Revelation. For the author brings his book to an end with a blunt warning against any kind of tampering whatsoever:

> I warn every man that heareth the words of the prophecy of this book that if any man shall add unto these things, God shall add unto him the plagues that are written in this book; and if any man shall take anything away from the words of the book of this prophecy, God shall take away his part out of the book of life and out of the holy city. (Rev. 22:18–19)

The use of a curse of this kind was a standard literary device of the period to make sure that the book was preserved through generations of copyists in exactly the same form in which it was written. When the Hebrew Scriptures were formally translated into Greek in the second century B.C., the same sort of curse was placed at the end of the translation and approved of as "a very wise precaution to ensure that the book might be preserved for all future time unchanged."[2]

If the arrangement and wording of the Book of Revelation are left unchanged, as the author requested, it is impossible to work out any literal interpretation of the events that are described. The author is not describing a literal, physical Day of Judgment, and there is no way in which his book can be forced into any such interpretation.

The second question that has bothered the scholars is the identity of the author himself. The whole weight of early literary tradition gives the authorship to John, the disciple whom Jesus loved, and from the first it was admitted into the church canon as his. The scholars are reluctant to agree to this, chiefly because they persist in their efforts to find a physical, literal interpretation that

---

[2] The quotation is from the *Letter of Aristeas*.

will fit the book and are quite rightly aware that such an interpreta-tion would never have found favor with John himself.

On the surface there is a great difference in wording between the Gospel of John and the Book of Revelation. Yet the fundamental idea behind the two books is exactly the same and is expressed elsewhere in the Bible only in the three letters that also are attributed to John.

All John's writings concern a single idea, the destruction of the darkness by the light. John wrote his gospel to prove that Jesus was the bringer of this light; and he wrote the Book of Revelation to record a subsequent warfare between light and darkness that ended only when the darkness was completely destroyed.

It is clear, therefore, why John's book cannot be made to fit into any interpretation which connects it with the other apocalypses of the period. John was not recording a physical destruction of the world in smoke and fire. He was recording a mental warfare, between the light which is the full knowledge of God and the darkness that is ignorance concerning him.

It is obvious to even the most casual reader that John did not put this account of the warfare between light and darkness into plain language. He wrote his book in symbols, constructing the most intricate combination of pictures and numbers to be found anywhere in the Bible.

The reason can be found in John's own experience. He wrote the fourth gospel in plain language and for a stated purpose: to prove that Jesus knew God. He saw the book become in his own day a breeding-ground for a series of esoteric, semi-Greek cults based on the Logos. Eventually also the fourth gospel served as the chief support of the bishops at Nicea when they officially decided, not that Jesus was "a man who has told you the truth he has heard from God" (John 8:40) but that he was in some mysterious way both God himself and also a sacrifice that God had accepted for the sins of the world.

Any clear statement of fact is immediately susceptible to misuse, and if the Book of Revelation had been put into plain language it would probably have been subject to more misuse than the fourth gospel. For the Book of Revelation is a book of prophecy, and there is nothing more dangerously delightful to the minds of human beings than a book that seems to foretell the future.

In spite of John's caution his book has been used for the last nineteen centuries by people determined to prove that the day of Armageddon had come whenever their private lives were upset by one of the wars or famines that recur so regularly throughout human history. The "beast" of the Book of Revelation has been identified over and over again by anxious citizens of every century as whatever distressed them most in their own day and loomed largest as a force of contemporary evil. The "666" of the beast has been fitted by ingenious ciphers to every tyrant from Nero to Hitler.

In each case, the interpretation can be made convincing as far as the immediate context is concerned. But no physical, historical interpretation can be fitted to the Book of Revelation as a whole. The device never works except when a few selected passages are isolated from the text and considered separately; and it was to prevent this that John pronounced a curse "if any man shall take anything away from the words of the book of this prophecy." (Rev. 22:19)

If the Book of Revelation is read as a whole, as it was intended to be read, it becomes a straightforward, orderly account of a spiritual warfare. It records what happens to the individual who accepts Jesus' discovery about God and who sets out to walk in the path that Jesus opened to him.

Jesus made a specific promise: "Whoever follows me will not have to walk in darkness but will have the light of life." (John 8:12) The Book of Revelation records the fulfillment of this promise.

For a complete understanding of John's account of the warfare between light and darkness, the reader should possess two qualifications.

The first of these, and by far the more important, is that the reader should understand what Jesus meant by eternal life. The book is addressed to the "servants" of God (Rev. 1:1) and John assumes that they all possess a common background of knowledge.

If a reader had no knowledge of music he would not pick up the score of a symphony and expect to understand what the series of marks on the paper were intended to represent. Without some training in the theory and practice of music, the symbols on paper become meaningless. There is no contact between the reader and the composer of the symphony, and the Fifth Symphony of Beethoven is nothing but a series of black marks set down apparently without order.

In the same way that the score of a symphony presupposes a knowledge of music in its readers, the Book of Revelation presupposes in its readers an accurate and to some extent a tested knowledge of the discovery of God that Jesus made. (Accurate, because his discovery of God was the full truth and no deviation from it is possible. Tested, because nothing really becomes a fact to the individual until he has found out that it can be proved.)

The Book of Revelation does not explain at any point what this discovery was. It assumes that this knowledge is already possessed by its readers, the "servants" of God (Rev. 1:1) for whom the book was written.

John wrote the book in the same way that Jesus spoke to his disciples the night of the Last Supper. That is to say, it is given as though to equals, and it is given in what Jesus called "figurative language." (John 16:25) John expected the meaning of his symbols to become clear as soon as the individual was far enough advanced on "the way that leads to life" (Matt. 7:14) to be able to use the book intelligently.

The second qualification that John takes for granted is less important than the first, but it is a useful one for his readers to possess. The book presupposes a thorough knowledge both of the Old Testament and of the various literary usages of John's own day.

John did not invent any of his symbols. He used a picture language that already existed. Each of the visions in the Book of Revelation is composed of a series of borrowed symbols, and it is desirable to know something of the original meaning of these symbols in order to understand the use to which John was putting them.

For instance, in the course of the first vision there is a description of a lamb with seven horns and seven eyes standing in the center of a colored throne. This is the equivalent, in ordinary language, of saying that Jesus was possessed of perfect strength and perfect vision and that the sacrifice involved in his crucifixion was one of perfect purity, the product of his knowledge that "The Father and I are one." (John 10:30) To reach this equivalent, however, the reader must be acquainted with the Book of Ezekiel, the fourth gospel, the procedure of the Jewish temple ritual, the accepted literary use of the word "horns" and the Hebrew theory of numbers.

John chose his symbols from various sources. Some of them, like the millennial kingdom and the lake of fire and the judgment of the dead, come from the apocalypses of his own day. Some, like the special meaning attached to certain numbers, come from ordinary contemporary usage. But the great majority come from the Hebrew Scriptures. There is hardly a book in the Old Testament, with the exception of brief stories like Ruth and Esther, that is not represented somewhere in John's book.

In most cases, John gives a symbolic meaning to what was originally intended as a literal picture. The lake of fire and the judgment of the dead were actual, physical facts to the men who wrote the apocalypses. Joel was writing about a real plague of locusts, and Ezekiel's measuring of the temple was intended to show the actual dimensions of a real building. But the Revelator takes over these literal pictures and uses them all as symbols instead.

John's book is constructed in such a way that his use of symbols, whether considered as individual pictures or as a narrative made up of these pictures, becomes nonsense if any of the symbols are taken literally. He apparently intended to make it impossible that the book should be taken literally and to force his readers to look instead for a unified, spiritual interpretation.

The Book of Revelation is constructed with intricate, almost mathematical precision, and as a logical whole. The use of symbols is consistent throughout, and the reader must resist the temptation to take any of them at face value. The book records a mental warfare, not a physical one, and the armies and cities of which John writes are symbols only. The saints that are killed under the altar, the idolaters that are cast into the burning lake, the horsemen that follow the word of God—these no more stand for specific men than Jerusalem and Babylon stand for real cities. Each is used as a symbol only, and the use is consistent.

The Book of Revelation may be summarized briefly as the account, in seven parts or visions, of the warfare between what Jesus called "the spirit of truth" (John 14:17) and what he called "a liar and the father of them." (John 8:44) This father of lies is symbolized in the Book of Revelation as the dragon "which deceiveth the whole world." (Rev. 12:9) There are seven stages whereby the dragon is first uncovered and then destroyed, until in the seventh vision the new Jerusalem, the city of the knowledge of truth, is the only place left in which to live.

The book is divided into seven visions because seven to the Hebrews was the number that symbolized completeness. It makes its first appearance in the Bible in the seven days of creation recorded in Genesis.

These seven visions are enclosed in a prologue and an epilogue. The prologue also divides into seven parts and is known as the Messages to the Seven Churches.

These messages to the seven churches are not admonitions from John himself. John's position throughout the book is not that of an author but of a transcriber. He is a man recording a revelation that came to him, "the revelation of Jesus Christ." (Rev. 1:1) Jesus was the only one who had experienced the warfare and the victory with which the Book of Revelation deals, and consequently he was the only one capable of giving a chart of "the way that leads to life." (Matt. 7:14)

John begins the book by picturing the coming of "Jesus Christ, who is the trustworthy witness," (Rev. 1:5) in a series of symbols that are used to emphasize two qualities: light and strength. "He had in his right hand seven stars . . . and his countenance was as the sun shineth in his strength." (Rev. 1:16) The picture as a whole is a composite of everything that is alien to darkness and weakness. Jesus came to John as he had come to Jerusalem, as one having authority.

The messages to the seven churches have been the subject of much controversy. Since all seven churches actually existed in Asia Minor when the Book of Revelation was written, it has been argued that John intended the messages to be merely local admonitions. This does not explain why the messages are placed in so formal and elaborate a framework. Nor does it explain why John chose to address only seven churches in his book, mentioning those in comparatively small towns like Thyatira and Philadelphia and neglecting some of the larger communities. Another kind of interpretation likes to see in the messages an actual foretelling of the course of church history through the next nineteen centuries, which is an attempt to pull the book down to the level of physical prophecy.

The seven churches, like everything else in the Book of Revelation, are symbols. Each one stands for a different aspect of ecclesiastical organization, of what happens when a group of people band themselves together to form a church. There are seven of these symbols to indicate the fact that with the seventh church the portrait of ecclesiasticism is complete.

(1) The church of Ephesus has had the intelligence to test all things for herself, and she has shown hard work and patience. But she is not as loving as she used to be, and this is a sin requiring such instant repentance that the church will disappear unless a change is made. But the individual who is victorious will eat of "the tree of life which is in the midst of the paradise of God." (Rev. 2:7)

(2) The church of Smyrna seems to be suffering distress and poverty and slander. She is nevertheless rich, and for her faithfulness

will receive the crown of life. And the individual who is victorious "shall not be hurt of the second death." (Rev. 2:11)

(3) The church of Pergamos has held fast to what she knew, but some of her members are committing the practices that lead to idolatry. They must repent quickly. But the individual who is victorious will receive "a white stone, and in the stone a new name written, which no man knoweth save he that receiveth it." (Rev. 2:17)

(4) The church of Thyatira has been loving and faithful and has worked hard. Nevertheless she has tolerated the "woman Jezebel" and whoever follows where the woman leads will be destroyed.[3] But the individual who is victorious will receive all power, "even as I received of my Father. And I will give him the morning star." (Rev. 2:27–28)

(5) The church of Sardis thinks she is alive but she is dead, since nothing she starts to do is ever fulfilled. She hears the word but does not obey it, and there are few white robes left in Sardis. But the individual who is victorious will hear his name proclaimed in the presence of God.

(6) The church of Philadelphia has a door opened before her which no man can close, and what little she possesses she has used to the full. She must hold fast and let no one take these things from her. And the individual who is victorious will be "a pillar in the temple of my God and he shall go no more out; and I will write upon him the name of my God and the name of the city of my God, which is new Jerusalem." (Rev. 3:12)

(7) The church of Laodicea is very proud of her wealth and her position in the world. "Thou sayest, 'I am rich and increased with goods and have need of nothing;' and knowest not that thou art wretched and miserable and poor and blind and naked. I counsel thee to buy of me gold tried in the fire . . . As many as I love I rebuke and chasten. Be earnest, therefore, and repent." (Rev. 3:17–19) But

---

[3]In 1 Kings, Jezebel was the queen who warred against Elijah.

the individual who is victorious will "sit with me on my throne, just as I also have been victorious and am set down with my Father on his throne." (Rev. 3:21)

"He that hath an ear, let him hear what the spirit saith unto the churches." (Rev. 3:22)

To understand the full force of these messages, it is important to observe upon what basis the churches are judged. According to the seven messages, the best thing that can happen to any group of people who organize themselves to honor God is poverty and struggle and the chance to show faithfulness under persecution. The worst thing that can happen to them is the attaining of wealth and power and the consequent growth of self-satisfaction.

Yet it is wealth and power that any organized group inevitably ends by wanting; and it is on this account that the seventh and final church, the ultimate portrait of ecclesiasticism, is so strongly condemned. It has achieved its purpose and has "need of nothing"; and it is the wrong purpose that it has achieved.

The second point to be noted about the seven messages is that it is not the group that is promised salvation but the individual. The warfare recorded in the Book of Revelation is not collective and it is never to the church that "victory" is promised. It is always to the individual.

This victory is the one that Jesus himself achieved. "To him that is victorious will I grant to sit with me on my throne." (Rev. 3:21) The victory consists of overcoming what Jesus called the devil and John called a dragon—the spirit of deceit that denies the allness of God. It consists of discovering the relationship to God that Jesus called sonship and John called the New Jerusalem—the complete awareness of union with the Father.

A detailed account of the stages of this warfare and the achievement of this victory is contained in the seven visions that make up the main part of the Book of Revelation. The visions are in chronological order. Each one records a further step in the development of the warfare, which continues until final victory is attained in the seventh vision. The individual has found for himself the city of God "and he shall go no more out." (Rev. 3:12)

THE FIRST VISION

The Book of Revelation is an account of the warfare between light and darkness, between the knowledge of God and the ignorance concerning him. It begins, logically enough, at the beginning, when the truth about God was first discovered.

This discovery was the one made by Jesus. The achievements of men like Moses and Elijah were of enormous importance, but Jesus was the first to discover a perfect God and a perfect creation. "God is light; there is no darkness in him at all." (I John 1:5)

The first vision in the Book of Revelation is a presentation, in a series of pictures, of the fact of this discovery. For the individual must realize that Jesus found the truth about God as the first step in his own warfare against darkness—the darkness of ignorance concerning God.

The discovery that Jesus made of "the only true God" (John 17:3) is portrayed by the Revelator in a series of symbols, most of which are derived from the first chapter of the Book of Ezekiel. The four winged creatures, the colored throne, the radiant halo, the crystal sea and the tumult of thunder are all pictures borrowed from the earlier prophet. And they combine to mean exactly what Ezekiel himself said they meant: "the semblance of the likeness of the glory of God." (Ezekiel 1:28)

In the right hand of the being on the throne there is a scroll whose contents are a mystery. It is sealed with seven seals and "no man was found worthy to open and to read the book, neither to look thereon." (Rev. 5:4)

The Revelator is overcome with sorrow that no one can read the scroll and is told, "Weep not. Behold, the lion of the tribe of Judah, of the line of David, has been victorious, so that he can open the scroll and loose the seven seals." (Rev. 5:5) This description of Jesus emphasizes one aspect about him that seemed important to John, his descent through the line of David and of other prophets who had loved God. A second aspect of Jesus is described in the next verse.

"And I beheld, and lo, in the midst of the throne . . . stood a Lamb as it had been slain, having seven horns and seven eyes." (Rev. 5:6) This second title that is given Jesus is a reference to his crucifixion, and here the Revelator is borrowing his symbolism from Jewish ritual. In the temple services, a lamb without blemish was offered as a sacrifice on the annual Day of Atonement. Jesus accepted the test of the crucifixion to prove literally his at-one-ment with the Father.

The fact that the Lamb stands in the midst of the throne is a reference to the statement on which Jesus based his life. "The Father and I are one." (John 10:30) The fact that the Lamb has seven horns is a reference to a current literary synonym for strength, originating from the horns that made the wild ox so powerful. "Seven horns" means perfect strength and "seven eyes" means perfect seeing.

This being comes and takes the scroll out of the "right hand of him that sat upon the throne" (Rev. 5:7) and a great cry of rejoicing goes up in acknowledgment of this act. "Thou hast made us unto our God kings and priests; and we shall reign on the earth." (Rev. 5:10) It is the immediate conviction of the individual, once he learns what Jesus discovered, that he himself is going to have control over evil and exert the same authority that Jesus did. "We shall reign."

THE SECOND VISION

The second vision in the Book of Revelation records what happens when the seven seals of the scroll are opened. The first four seals are opened and four horses are revealed, white, red, black and grey. These colored horses come originally from the sixth chapter of the Book of Zechariah.

In most interpretations of the Book of Revelation these four horsemen are rather vaguely grouped together and labeled pestilence, war, famine and death. The text supports the last three interpretations but there is nothing to indicate that the first horseman stands for pestilence. The symbols used here are the symbols of victory. "And I saw, and behold a white horse, and he that sat on him had a bow; and a crown was given unto him, and he went forth conquering and to conquer." (Rev. 6:2)

This rider on a white horse that symbolizes victory is the natural result of the end of the preceding vision. "We shall reign." The individual has agreed to the truth of Jesus' discovery about God, and therefore he assumes that his own victory over anything unlike God should follow immediately.

The reason it does not is that this sense of victory is as yet wholly untested and untried. The truth of Jesus' discovery has been accepted theoretically, not as an unassailable fact. And therefore on the heels of the first horseman, the easy assumption of victory over all evil, come various forms of evil, all plainly unconquered.

The opening of the second seal brings War, on a horse that "was red; and power was given to him that sat thereon to take peace from the earth, that men should slaughter one another." (Rev. 6:4) The opening of the third seal brings Famine, a rider on a black horse with a pair of scales in his hand and a voice speaking of the scarcity of wheat. The opening of the fourth seal brings a grey horse, "and his name that sat on him was Death." (Rev. 6:8)

These three horsemen—death by violence, death by lack and death itself—symbolize the weight of the visible world continually contradicting Jesus' discovery of a perfect creation. By their presence they proclaim that the world cannot have been made in the image and likeness of God. They proclaim that the basis of the world is not life but death and that all living things are born only to die. It is impossible that God is life; they themselves have full power over both life and death, and death reigns.

The fifth seal is opened and a great cry goes up against the power and the permanence of death. How long will the three horsemen be able "to kill with sword and with hunger and with death"? (Rev. 6:8)

"How long, O Lord?" (Rev. 6:10) This cry is uttered by "the souls of them that were slain for the word of God, and for the testimony which they held." (Rev. 6:9)

These souls under the altar that have been "slain" for adhering to the truth correspond to the "saints" that appear elsewhere in the Book of Revelation. Both stand as symbols of the highest aspect of human endeavor and typify the highest and holiest achievement of which the human mind is capable.

At this point in the development of the warfare, the highest aspect of concentrated human endeavor has acknowledged that Jesus had proved death to be powerless against a correct understanding of God. It was to be expected that victory over death would follow this acknowledgment. Instead it is a heightened awareness of death that has followed, an awareness of the multitude of ways in which it apparently has power to contradict the fact that God is life.

In answer to the cry, "How long, O Lord?" the souls under the altar are told to "rest yet for a little season, until their fellow-servants and their brethren, that should be killed as they were, should be fulfilled." (Rev. 6:11) There is to be no fulfillment until everything has been, as they were, "slain for the word of God." (Rev. 6:9)

Why human endeavor should have to be "slain" before God can be recognized as *all* is a question that could be answered theoretically at any time: all effort to get back to God implies a state of separation from God, and is therefore based on a belief in Jesus' discovery rather than a full understanding of it. But the practical answer to the question is given in the sixth vision. In the sixth vision the final enemy, the belief in separation from God, is overthrown, and it is the successive victories of the preceding visions that make this overthrow possible. In the second vision this final enemy has not even been discovered, much less overthrown.

The second vision continues with the opening of the sixth seal, which ushers in "a great earthquake." (Rev. 6:12)

The symbol of an earthquake occurs more than once in the Book of Revelation and always to indicate a shaking-up and overturning of former beliefs. In this case what is overturned is a belief in the stability and permanence of physical law.

To make this clear John chooses a series of symbols that typify light and regularity and order, and then has the earthquake deprive them of these properties. The sun, the symbol of unfailing light, becomes black as sackcloth. The stars, the symbol of perfect order, scatter like unripe figs in a high wind. The mountains, the symbol of unswerving stability, are moved out of their places. And the kings of the earth, the symbol of unquestioned authority, grovel among the rocks.

In other words, the earthquake symbolizes the discovery that nothing in all the world can be trusted to possess light or security or permanence. There is no safety to be found anywhere in the things of the world. It is the spirit only that gives life.

This safety that can be found only in God is symbolized by the Revelator as "an angel ascending from the east" like a sunrise. (Rev. 7:2) The angel bears in his hand "the seal of the living God" (Rev. 7:2) and orders that the coming warfare shall not begin until all the servants of God have been sealed on their foreheads.

The "seal" is an accepted Old Testament sign of possession and protection. It is used here to establish the fact that the servant of God, the man who has set out on the long warfare to find God, is God's own. However savage the coming warfare may seem to be, there is nothing in it that can injure the servant of God as long as he remembers what his identity is.

According to the Revelator, it is the twelve tribes of Israel who are sealed in this manner. "Israel" means "striver with God" in the original Hebrew. This was a title of honor that was given to Jacob (Genesis 32:28) because he strove all one night with what came to him and refused to let it go until he had discovered its real name and it had blessed him. The descendant of Israel is whoever does what Jacob did.

Twelve thousand are chosen from each of the twelve tribes, or descendants of Israel, a double emphasis on the number twelve. The number seven was used by the Hebrews to symbolize completeness, but it could be any kind of completeness, good or bad. The horns of the Lamb are seven, for instance, but so are the heads of the beast. The number twelve, on the other hand, always symbolized holy completeness and is not used in the Book of Revelation in any other sense.

John's symbol of twelve thousand from each of the twelve tribes of Israel means, therefore, complete and holy kinship with the spirit that earned Jacob his title of Israel, the spirit that is willing to declare to whatever comes as consciousness, "I will not let you go unless you bless me." (Genesis 32:26)

Then the Revelator describes a "great multitude, which no man could number, of all nations and kindreds and peoples and tongues." (Rev. 7:9) All of them wear white robes and stand before the throne of God to "serve him day and night in his temple." (Rev. 7:15)

This is the direct result of the sealing of Israel that has just taken place. For as soon as the individual earns the title of Israel by steadfastly redeeming what comes to him as consciousness, he learns that everything that comes to him as consciousness— "nations and kindreds and peoples and tongues"—is proclaiming the glory of God.

With the realization of this comes the breaking of the seventh seal. A great peace descends. Nothing seems to be left to do except to recognize the fact that God is all and give him glory.

The seven seals have been opened. God has been revealed as the only authority, the only protection and the only reality. There is silence in heaven, and the prayers of the saints mingle with the incense of praise "upon the golden altar which was before the throne." (Rev. 8:3)

THE THIRD VISION

This holy silence of praise and of the awareness of God endures, according to the Revelator, for "about the space of half an hour." (Rev. 8:1) In other words, it lasts for a very short time.

Mental quiet is not victory. Truth acknowledged is not truth proven. The kingdom of heaven that Jesus taught is not a momentary certainty that God is all, but the tested, permanent conviction of that fact. "For the reign of God is not a matter of words but of power." (I Cor. 4:20)

This power is achieved, not through peace but through warfare. It is this warfare with which the subsequent visions in the Book of Revelation deal.

Once the warfare is begun there can be no truce. As Jesus said, no one is worthy of the kingdom of heaven who puts his hand to the plow and then looks back. The destruction of ignorance concerning God (which is the only thing that can be destroyed) must grow increasingly comprehensive until there is nothing left to destroy—until the complete and perfect knowledge of God, which Jesus called the kingdom of heaven, is all that remains.

It is in the third vision of the Book of Revelation that the warfare actually begins. Nevertheless, it was the revelation of truth recorded in the first two visions that precipitated the conflict. Or, to use John's symbolism, it is fire from the altar of God that causes the great earthquake that now shakes the earth. (Rev. 8:5)

In the same way that the revelation of the second vision was symbolized by the opening of seven seals, the warfare of the third vision is symbolized by the sounding of seven trumpets.

There is nothing in the least easy or comfortable about the events that the seven trumpets herald. As Jesus emphasized throughout his ministry, the finding of the kingdom of heaven is not a peaceful experience. "The gate is narrow and the road is hard that leads to life, and there are few that find it." (Matt. 7:14) "Do not think that I have come to bring peace to the earth. I have not come to bring peace, but a sword." (Matt. 10:34)

The Revelator underlines the intensity of this warfare in the symbols he uses to describe the results of the sounding of the first four trumpets. When the first sounds, a third of the trees and all green things are destroyed by fire. When the second sounds, a third of the life in the sea is destroyed when the waters turn to blood. When the third sounds, a third of the rivers and fountains are poisoned by a star called Wormwood. When the fourth sounds, a third of the sun, moon and stars are darkened into night.

There are three points to be noticed in John's description of the sounding of these trumpets. The first is the emphasis the Revelator puts on the fact that it is always "one-third" that is affected. The terror never becomes complete; that is to say, the individual is never entirely overcome.

The second point to be noticed is the identity of those who sound the trumpets: they are "angels which stood before God." (Rev. 8:2) It will be remembered that the purpose of the warfare is the destruction of ignorance concerning God. However terrifying and even inexplicable the warfare may seem to the individual in some of its earlier stages, it is nevertheless the way he learns. It is not he that is destroyed but his ignorance. Therefore, since destruction of ignorance is to be the outcome of the warfare, the power that precipitates it is not evil. In John's symbolism, it is the seven angels who stand before God that blow the seven trumpets.

The third point to be noticed is the special identity of the angels who blow the first four trumpets. These are the four angels that were held in check in the preceding vision until the servants of God, the descendants of Israel, could be sealed on their foreheads. The angel that did the sealing "cried with a loud voice to the four angels to whom it was given to hurt the earth and the sea, saying, 'Hurt not the earth, neither the sea, nor the trees, till we have sealed the servants of our God.'" (Rev. 7:2–3) In other words, the warfare does not begin until the servant of God knows enough to protect himself from it so that he cannot be overcome.

The same point is brought out even more clearly in the sounding of the fifth trumpet. This evokes from a bottomless pit a swarm that is reminiscent of the locusts in Joel but much more terrifying, strange armed creatures with the teeth of lions and led by Apollyon. These are symbols of mental evil rather than physical; for "it was commanded them that they should not hurt the grass of the earth, neither any green thing, neither any tree; but only those men which have not the seal of God." (Rev. 9:4)

The sounding of the sixth trumpet evokes another form of destruction, a troop of armed horsemen that ride forth to murder with fire and smoke and brimstone the men of the earth who "worship devils and idols." (Rev. 9:20) These "men" are not individual human beings. They symbolize the impulse of the human mind towards idolatry, towards the desire to give honor and authority to some power that is not the power of God. One-third of these men are killed by the horsemen. In other words, the terror these horsemen represent kills in the individual at least a part of his love for idolatry and forces him to concentrate himself on the fact that God is all.

The seventh trumpet does not yet sound. Instead, a mighty angel appears to explain what will happen when the seventh trumpet is sounded. "The angel which I saw stand upon the sea and upon the earth lifted up his hand to heaven and sware by him that liveth for ever and ever, who created heaven and the things that are therein, and the earth and the things that are therein, and the sea and the things that are therein, that there should be delay no longer; but in the days of the voice of the seventh angel, when he shall begin to sound, the mystery of God should be finished." (Rev. 10:5–7)

This angel who stands upon earth and sea is described in the symbols John habitually uses for spiritual illumination: sun and fire. Over his head there is a rainbow, a reference to the use of the rainbow in Genesis as a token of a covenant between God and man. "And God said, 'This is the token of the covenant which I make between me and you . . . It shall come to pass, when I bring a cloud over the earth, that the bow shall be seen in the cloud.' " (Gen. 9:12–14) Like the rainbow in Genesis, John's angel is "clothed with a cloud," (Rev. 10:1) an example of the precision with which John was able to bend Old Testament symbols to his own use. For it is out of the storm that the light comes, enduring after the storm is over.

The right hand of the angel holds a "little book" that is open. This symbol of the open book comes from the third chapter in Ezekiel, and from Ezekiel also is the description of the book that follows. It is sweet to the taste but it is very bitter to digest.

A book is a record or testimony, and the fact that this book is in the hand of an angel means that it symbolizes a record of the truth about God. This description does not fit the Bible itself, which is not so much a record of the truth about God as a record of the way this truth was ultimately found. Even the fourth gospel, which is the only one to give a clear record of what Jesus taught, does not explain the principle upon which he based his teaching. The first such explanation is the one given in the chapter called "Recapitulation" in *Science and Health With Key to the Scriptures* by Mary Baker Eddy.

The appearance of the little book in the hand of the angel has nothing whatever to do with the date on which Mrs. Eddy wrote this chapter. The Book of Revelation is not dealing with physical, historical events. What is being described here is a moment that is the direct result of the warfare that has gone before, the moment in which the contents of the chapter becomes an "open book" and it is understood to be neither a system of healing nor a comfortable creed, but an exact statement of an exact fact.

The prophet is given the open book to eat, and he finds it sweet to the taste but bitter to digest. The individual finds it delightful to accept the general proposition that God is all. But he finds it less easy to accept the responsibility that such an agreement demands and be willing to maintain the truth when the whole of the visible world rises up to brand it as a lie.

The ministry of Jesus consisted of his ability to prove what he said, and he expected his followers to do the same. "I tell you, whoever believes in me will do such things as I do, and things greater yet." (John 14:12) This ability to prove the truth is the subject of the Revelator's next picture, and until it occurs the seventh trumpet cannot sound.

John begins his picture with a symbol taken from the last chapter of Ezekiel. Ezekiel is describing the measuring of the temple, and states that the presence of this temple within the city walls gives the city a title: "The Lord is there." (Ezekiel 48:35) It is this temple, therefore, that ensures the presence of God in the city.

What ensures the presence of God is the fact that God is all, and it is in this sense that the Revelator uses Ezekiel's temple and describes the measuring of "the temple of God." (Rev. 11:1) The temple is the fact that God is *all,* and the "measuring" is the awareness of that fact. The outer court, however, cannot be measured, "for it is given unto the heathen." (Rev. 11:2)

These heathen do not stand for any group of men, any more than do the "idolaters" that were destroyed with the sounding of the sixth trumpet. They stand for unbelief, for the inability to believe that God is all when the evidence of the whole visible world is so obviously to the contrary.

The unbelief is destroyed by the power of truth. And this power the truth possesses, the ability to prove itself visibly in the world, is symbolized by what John calls the "two witnesses." (Rev. 11:3)

The two witnesses originate in the Book of Zechariah, and John is quoting from Zechariah when he says the two witnesses "are the two olive trees and the two candlesticks standing before the God of the earth." (Rev. 11:4) It is the "God of the earth" they stand before rather than the God of heaven because these two witnesses are concerned solely with the power of the truth to manifest itself "on earth," that is, visibly.

It is worth noticing how the prophet Zechariah originally characterized the two witnesses. Zechariah asked who they were and was given this for an answer: "Not by might, nor by power, but by my spirit, saith the Lord." (Zechariah 4:6) It is this power of the spirit that John is evoking in his picture of the two witnesses, the power that Jesus called "the spirit of truth." (John 14:17)

The Revelator continues his portrait of the two witnesses by linking them up with the two greatest Old Testament prophets. He says the two witnesses "have power to shut heaven, that it rain not in the days of their prophecy, and have power over waters to turn them to blood." (Rev. 11:6) It was Elijah who had power to prevent rain (I Kings 17:1) and it was Moses who turned water to blood. (Exodus 7:19)

This direct reference to Elijah and Moses is not to be taken literally. It is not to the men themselves that John is referring but to the quality that made them great prophets. Moses and Elijah were the two great prophets before Jesus who were able to prove what they said.[4]

It is this quality that is possessed also by the two witnesses, who are symbols of the ability of the spirit of truth to prove itself visibly. They bear witness that the truth, because it is the truth, can be proven—that the God who is God of heaven is also "God of the earth." (Rev. 11:4)

Against this testimony to the authority of the spirit of truth is ranged the tremendous power of material law, which completely contradicts the authority to which the two witnesses testify. John's symbol for the power of material law is a "beast." This beast rises up out of a pit to make war against the two witnesses and succeeds in killing them.

"When they shall have finished their testimony, the beast that ascendeth out of the bottomless pit shall make war against them, and shall overcome them and kill them. And their dead bodies shall lie in the street of the great city which spiritually is called Sodom and Egypt, where also our Lord was crucified." (Rev. 11:7–8)

The word "city" appears in three different ways in the Book of Revelation, each time describing a different kind of mental state. Here the frame of mind that is being described is the inclination of the individual to believe what he sees. It is the habit of judging "externally," as Jesus called it. (John 7:24)

---

[4] See the discussion of Elijah in Chapter VI of *The Search For God,* especially pp. 118–119.

It was in this "city" that Jesus was crucified. He repeatedly told his disciples that he was not going to his death but to prove the existence of life. Yet to outward appearances he died, and it seemed clear to those who believed the evidence of their own eyes that the man who had denied the authority of material law had finally been conquered by it.

It is in this same "city" that the two witnesses appear to have been conquered by the beast. Those that live "upon the earth" are delighted, for the witnesses have been a torment to them by insisting on an authority that is not a visible authority. "They that dwell upon the earth shall rejoice over them and make merry . . . because these two prophets tormented them that dwelt on the earth." (Rev. 11:10) Those who live in the city "which spiritually is called Sodom and Egypt" are very comfortable in their unquestioning acceptance of material testimony and do not wish to be disturbed.

The death of the two witnesses lasts for "three days and a half." (Rev. 11:11) John might have been expected to use the number three, which was the resurrection number. But for some reason "three and a half" had definitely come to mean for New Testament writers a period of testing. Both Luke and James give this figure as the duration of Elijah's drought (Luke 4:25, James 5:17), although there is nothing to that effect in the Old Testament.

After the period of testing, the authority of the two witnesses is triumphantly established. "After three days and a half the spirit of life from God entered them and they stood upon their feet." (Rev. 11:11) The case is the same as with the crucifixion of Jesus. The whole force of material law has achieved nothing except to give the two witnesses a chance to prove the reality of their message. The apparent victory of the beast only serves, in the end, to testify to "the spirit of life from God."

With the resurrection of the two witnesses, a great change comes over the "city" that believed them to be dead. It is still the same city, still convinced by the testimony of its own eyes. But now the eyes give testimony to life rather than death, to the power of the spirit rather than the power of the beast. Anything that is not willing to acknowledge the power of the spirit is destroyed in the city, under the symbolism of an earthquake destroying seven thousand men and the rest giving "glory to the God of heaven." (Rev. 11:13)

At last the seventh trumpet can be sounded, the long delayed trumpet that will bring to an end the "mystery of God." (Rev. 10:7) Through the two witnesses it has been shown that the words in the open book do not express a theory. They express a fact. The power of the spirit of truth is literally the only power there is and nothing can stand against it. What is acknowledged "in heaven" can be proven "on earth."

This is the fact that all the hosts of heaven proclaim with a mighty shout as soon as the seventh trumpet has sounded:

> The kingdoms of this world are become the kingdoms of our Lord and of his Christ, and he shall reign for ever and ever. (Rev. 11:15)

God and the understanding of God has complete sovereignty over the whole earth. "We give thee thanks, O Lord God Almighty . . . because thou hast taken to thyself thy great power and hast reigned." (Rev. 11:17)

The vision closes with a formula that John took from the apocalypses. "Thy wrath is come, and the time of the dead, that they should be judged, and that thou shouldst give reward unto thy servants the prophets and to the saints and them that fear thy name." (Rev. 11:18) This formula was used in apocalyptic literature as a sign of the end of the world, and it is in that sense that John uses it here. It is no more to be taken literally than Zechariah's lampstands and olive trees.

John uses the formula as a symbol to record the end of the old way of looking at the world. The earth is no longer what it was. It has been acknowledged to be the manifestation of the presence and the glory of God. "Thou hast taken to thyself thy great power and hast reigned." (Rev. 11:17)

THE FOURTH VISION

The fourth vision is the direct result of the third. It records what happens once the discovery that God is all is accepted as a literal fact rather than as a theoretical abstraction.

It will be remembered that the Book of Revelation is an account of the warfare between light and darkness, between the spirit of truth and the spirit of deceit. The spirit of truth has already been discovered. The next step is the uncovering of the spirit of deceit, the ignorance about God that Jesus called "a liar and the father of them" (John 8:44) and which John calls "the great dragon . . . which deceiveth the whole world." (Rev. 12:9)

The uncovering of this dragon, the adversary with which all the subsequent warfare in the Book of Revelation is to deal, is brought about by the birth of understanding. And John presents the birth of understanding under the symbol of a woman giving birth to a child.

The idea of a woman in labor as the symbol of a mind in travail is used constantly by the Old Testament prophets. Isaiah in particular liked the image, just as he liked the symbol of a child who would rule the nations with a rod of iron. The Revelator combines Isaiah's two images in his account of the woman who gives birth to a son.

In describing the woman, John again uses the symbols that stand for spiritual illumination. She is "clothed with the sun, and the moon under her feet, and upon her head a crown of twelve stars." (Rev. 12:1)

Standing before the woman, waiting to devour the child as soon as it is born, stands the great antagonist with whose destruction the rest of the Book of Revelation deals, the destroyer of the earth that must himself be destroyed before the kingdom of God can be made manifest. John pictures him as a tremendous force, "a great red dragon having seven heads and ten horns and seven crowns upon his heads." (Rev. 12:3)

The symbol of a dragon is not derived from the Old Testament prophets, in whose writings the word appears only occasionally and never in just this connection. The Revelator has gone further back, to the talking serpent of the Book of Genesis.

The enmity between the woman and the dragon is derived from Genesis also, and it is a fitting symbolism that the talking serpent in the first book of the Bible, who is promised warfare with the seed of the woman, should appear in the last book of the Bible at the climax of the warfare.

The dragon hopes to devour the child as soon as it is born, for if the child succeeds in getting sovereignty over the world the rule of the dragon is over. "The dragon stood before the woman which was ready to be delivered, for to devour her child as soon as it was born. And she brought forth a man child who was to rule all nations with a rod of iron; and her child was caught up unto God and to his throne." (Rev. 12:4–5) The child stands for the understanding of God and is instantly protected from lies by the fact of its own identity.

Then a great war breaks out "in heaven"—in the place where the understanding of God has been enthroned. "There was war in heaven; Michael and his angels fought against the dragon; and the dragon fought, and his angels, and prevailed not; neither was their place found any more in heaven." (Rev. 12:7–8)

Once the dragon is cast out of heaven he cannot return to it. In the place where the man child, the understanding of God, is enthroned, the spirit of deceit has lost its place and its authority and will never be able to regain them again.

Up to this point the statements of the dragon have been believed in as the truth. But now, with the birth of understanding, he is known to be a liar, and it is as such that the Revelator defines him.

John says that the dragon is "that old serpent, called the devil and Satan, which deceiveth the whole world." (Rev. 12:9) He also calls him "the accuser of our brethren . . . which accused them before our God day and night." (Rev. 12:10) This is the equivalent of the definition that Jesus gave: "He was a murderer from the first, and he has nothing to do with the truth, for there is no truth in him. When he tells a lie he speaks in his true character, for he is a liar and the father of them." (John 8:44)

The casting of the dragon out of heaven symbolizes the point in the warfare when for the first time the dragon is seen for what he really is, a deceiver. This great, crowned power has previously been honored as reality. His accusations against the sons of the living God have been respectfully received as the truth and the world has been admitted to be made up of dying men. Now it is realized for the first time that the cause of death is the dragon—ignorance concerning God—the killer that "was a murderer from the first." (John 8:44)

This discovery is the result of the sounding of the seventh trumpet in the preceding vision. This symbolized the discovery that "the kingdoms of the world" are the kingdoms of God and the sovereignty over them is his only. The earth is not something that must be exalted or altered or destroyed in order to make the kingdom of God manifest. The earth is already the kingdom of God, the holy manifestation of his presence. It is only the "deceiver" that makes it appear to be otherwise.

It is the deceiver, the murderer from the beginning, who maintains that the world is made up of millions of bewildered minds locked up in bodies of dying clay. He accuses the sons of the living God "day and night" (Rev. 12:10) and up to this point he has been successful in his accusation. Now he is successful no longer. Once the understanding of God is born and it is realized that the world is made in his image, the dragon can no longer maintain himself as a reality. He is exposed as a lie, having "nothing to do with the truth, for there is no truth in him." (John 8:44)

The first step in the warfare against the dragon is this victory "in heaven," the victory that strips him of his claim to be telling the truth and brands him as a deceiver. The victory in heaven does not destroy the dragon, but it takes away the basis of his authority. Never again is he honored as reality. He is understood to be a deceiver and is so named.

The second step in the warfare against the dragon is the warfare "on earth," and this lasts a much longer time. It is one thing to grasp a fact intellectually or emotionally, and quite another thing to acknowledge it practically as the whole of reality.

Nevertheless, once the first battle is won, the winning of the second becomes inevitable. "Now is come salvation, and strength, and the kingdom of our God, and the power of his Christ; for the accuser of our brethren is cast down, which accused them before our God day and night." (Rev. 12:10) The dragon sets himself to the warfare upon earth in "great wrath, because he knoweth that he hath but a short time." (Rev. 12:12)

The dragon is not able to declare open war on earth, for the spirit of deceit can only hope to operate successfully as long as it remains hidden. Therefore he delegates his authority, in this stage of the warfare, to two other beings. One of these delegates John calls the "beast" and the other he calls the "false prophet." (Rev. 16:13)

The beast, the symbol of material law, has already made an appearance in an earlier vision in the Book of Revelation when it tried to destroy the two witnesses. But now the position of the beast has changed. With the birth of understanding it is now clear that the beast has no authority of its own. It derives its authority directly from the dragon, the father of lies. The beast possesses nothing of itself; it was "the dragon gave him his power, and his seat, and great authority." (Rev. 13:2) In other words, it is through ignorance concerning God that material law gets any power, and this is the only way in which it can be credited with "great authority."

What is true of material law at this point was equally true of the beast on its earlier appearance in the Book of Revelation. It was always "the dragon which gave power unto the beast." (Rev. 13:4) But at the time of the third vision the identity of the beast was not yet understood. It was not until the warfare in heaven that material law was understood to derive its whole power from a lie.

John describes the beast in a series of pictures taken from the Book of Daniel and has chosen his symbols to underline the enormous power that the beast has succeeded in acquiring through the activities of the deceiver. The beast has the feet of a bear and the mouth of a lion. Like the dragon, it has seven heads and is armed with ten horns; "and upon his heads the name of blasphemy." (Rev. 13:1)

The respect that the beast commands on earth is very great. "All the earth followed the beast in wonder. And they worshiped the dragon which gave power unto the beast; and they worshiped the beast, saying, 'Who is like unto the beast? Who is able to make war with him?' " (Rev. 13:3–4)

What is like the power of material law, which can take away supply by an absence of bread, health by an alteration of tissue, or life by a bullet? Who is able to war with the fact that all men are born with the seeds of death in them, created of dust and returning to dust? Who can defy the beast and its wholesale denial that God is life, the beast which unceasingly raises its voice "in blasphemy against God, to blaspheme his name and his tabernacle and them that dwell in heaven"? (Rev. 13:6)

The highest aspect of human endeavor is helpless against the entrenched power of material law. As the Revelator puts it, "it was given unto him to make war with the saints and to overcome them." (Rev. 13:7) There is only one way to war successfully with the beast and that is to war with the dragon—in other words, to refuse to be deceived.

The beast is a delegate only. It gets its power from the dragon, ignorance concerning God, and this power operates hypnotically to convince its worshipers of the reality of what is actually a lie. It is the deceiver that has given the beast its "great authority" (Rev. 13:2) and it is the deceiver that must be attacked and overcome. To fight effect with effect is useless. "He that killeth with the sword must be killed by the sword." (Rev. 13:10) The sword is the beast's own weapon, and if it is met on its own ground it cannot be destroyed.

The dragon has a second delegate which also operates on earth. This is a second beast to which the Revelator later gives the title of the "false prophet." (Rev. 16:13)

John describes this false prophet in a curious way. He has "horns like a lamb." (Rev. 13:11) The only use of the symbol of the lamb elsewhere in the Book of Revelation is in reference to Jesus, and "horns" are always used as a symbol of power. Therefore the

Revelator's phrase means that the false prophet is apparently able to exert the same power that Jesus exerted.

The Revelator also says of the false prophet, "He doeth great wonders, so that he maketh fire come down from heaven on the earth in the sight of men." (Rev. 13:13) The bringing down of fire from heaven is a reference to the conviction in the Old Testament days that this was a sure sign that the prophet was sent from God. It was this test of a prophet's credentials that Elijah suggested when he was competing against the four hundred and fifty prophets of Baal. "The god who answers by fire, he is God." (I Kings 18:24)

The false prophet has the power to do "miracles." He can apparently exert the power that Elijah and Jesus exerted, the power that raised the dead and cured cripples and gave eyes to the blind. This is also the power that was exerted by the "two witnesses" earlier in the Book of Revelation, but this prophet is not in the least like the two witnesses.

The false prophet can produce healings and he does it in the name of God. Nevertheless, this power is not based on a knowledge of God. It is rooted in ignorance concerning God; the false prophet is a delegate of the dragon.

John makes this point entirely clear. Although the prophet has the horns of a lamb, he speaks "as a dragon." (Rev. 13:11) He fights for the dragon at the battle of Armageddon (Rev. 16:13) and he is a true delegate of the father of lies. For the false prophet "deceiveth them that dwell on the earth by the means of those miracles which he has power to do." (Rev. 13:14)

The false prophet stands for the belief that human mentality can control material law, for the theory of "mind over matter." It stands for the belief that the human mind, if its faith is sufficiently great, can manipulate matter for its own ends.

The authority of the false prophet comes from the fact that it actually can produce results. If the faith in it is strong enough, mental healing is quite capable of producing "miracles."

Moreover, these miracles are usually credited to God. For the false prophet has the horns of a lamb, and mental healing always tries to pass itself off as God's delegate. "I can heal you, for God is all and you are well, since God creates neither sin, sickness nor death."

A statement of this kind sounds very well indeed, and if a healing results from it, it would seem obvious that the healing had "come down from heaven." (Rev. 13:13) It takes a very alert "servant of God" to realize that it is not knowledge of God that is operating here. It is ignorance of God operating through an emissary who "deceiveth them that dwell on earth by the means of those miracles which he has power to do." (Rev. 13:14)

The most alert servant of God since Jesus recognized clearly the quality of this deception.

> 'I can heal you, for God is all, and you are well, since God creates neither sin, sickness, nor death.' Such statements result in the sick either being healed by their faith in what you tell them—which heals only as a drug would heal, through belief—or in no effect whatever. If the faith-healer succeeds in securing (kindling) the belief of the patient in his own recovery, the practitioner will have performed a faith-cure which he mistakenly pronounces Christian Science.[5]

It would be extremely difficult to detect the false prophet, since it has the power of a "lamb" and can bring down fire from heaven and work miracles, except that there is one sure mark of identity. The false prophet is always in close cooperation with material law, always careful to give honor to the beast.

The authority of the false prophet rests in the belief that mind can dominate matter. Its sole effort, therefore, is always to change bad matter into good matter—to change lack into a comfortable bank balance and pain into pleasure. The "miracles which he had power to do" are "in the sight of the beast." (Rev. 13:14) That is to

---

[5] From an article called "Principle and Practice" by Mary Baker Eddy. First published in the *Christian Science Sentinel,* September 1, 1917, on page 10.

say, they never challenge the fundamental authority of the beast. They merely serve to manipulate that authority for their own ends.

The "two witnesses" challenged the fundamental authority of the beast when "the spirit of life from God entered into them" after they had been killed "and they stood upon their feet." (Rev. 11:11) This shook the world's faith in the power of the beast. But now the "deadly wound was healed, and all the world followed the beast in wonder." (Rev. 13:3) For the false prophet calls itself a true prophet and yet advocates worship of the beast, promising its worshipers that they can use the truth about God to get any material thing that they happen to want.

The false prophet is subtle enough to offer its temptation in the name of God: "It is right for you to have all these things, since God is all." But since God is all, there are obviously no "things" apart from him, either to acquire or rule over; and to think that there are is to do homage, however unconsciously, to the devil.

The false prophet promises many things. But it promises above all, since it is able to manipulate matter, that it can guarantee safety to anyone that will believe in it. The Revelator symbolizes this by a mark which the false prophet can place on the right hand or on the forehead, in imitation of the seal on the forehead that was given the sons of Israel. "And no man might buy or sell [that is, live comfortably in the world] save he that had the mark, or the name of the beast, or the number of his name." (Rev. 13:17)

But the delegate of the dragon cannot fulfill its own promise. The Revelator gives the "number of the beast" and it is at once clear that the seal is only an imitation of the real one and the protection it offers is unreal. For the mark of the beast, the number of his name, is 666. (Rev. 13:18) This is the number that three times tries to reach seven (the symbol of any kind of completeness whatsoever) and three times fails.

In order to emphasize the full force of this number, the Revelator contrasts it in the next sentence with the number of those who have the "Father's name written in their foreheads." (Rev. 14:1) The number of these is 144,000. Twelve is the number that symbolizes perfect completeness, and this number is twelve multiplied twelve thousand times.

These are the sons of Israel who were sealed in the course of the second vision. They "follow the Lamb whithersoever he goeth" (Rev. 14:4) and for that reason are protected by his Father's name. "They are virgins" (here a symbol of mental purity) and "they have never been known to utter a lie." (Rev. 14:5) This means that they have no intercourse with the false prophet, who is a liar, or with the dragon, who is the father of lies.

The spirit that this multiple of twelve symbolizes—the wholeness of spirit that honors God only—refuses to be deceived by the claims of the dragon and of his two delegates. It is aware that there is no power apart from God. Therefore, there is really no warfare going on between opposing powers, since God is all and there is nothing to oppose him. All that is needed is to refuse to honor the spirit of deceit and to honor instead the spirit of truth. "And they sung as it were a new song before the throne . . . and no man could learn that song except the hundred and forty and four thousand which were redeemed from the earth." (Rev. 14:3)

The "new song," the conviction that victory is already won, is symbolized by the Revelator as three angels flying "in the midst of heaven" (Rev. 14:6) to announce as having already occurred what has not yet taken place.

The first angel, who possesses "the everlasting gospel to preach to them that dwell on the earth" (Rev. 14:6) proclaims that the day of God's judgment has arrived. The second angel announces that Babylon has fallen. And the third angel gives the lie to the claim of the false prophet that those who worship the beast will be protected. "They have no rest day and night, who worship the beast and his image." (Rev. 14:11)

Then the Revelator hears a voice from heaven saying, "Blessed are the dead which die in the Lord." (Rev. 14:13) Blessed are those who have died to the old way of life, who "have died with Christ to a material way of looking at things." (Colossians 2:20) "Yes, saith the spirit, they may rest from their labors." (Rev. 14:13)

Those who have died to a material way of looking at things are no longer obliged to war with the beast. They know that the beast has no real authority and they give him none. Moreover, they can prove he has no real authority, for "their works do follow them." (Rev. 14:13)

THE FIFTH VISION

The fifth vision records the intensification of the warfare, under the symbolism of the "seven angels having the seven last plagues." (Rev. 15:1)

These seven plagues have a single purpose: to destroy any desire to worship the beast. The plagues are all directed against the men who have the mark of the beast upon them to force them to "repent," or, to give a more literal translation of the Greek word, to make them change their minds.

In order to emphasize that the ultimate purpose of the seven plagues is purification, not destruction, the Revelator precedes his account of them with two symbols taken from harvesting.

These two symbols were both favorites of the Old Testament prophets, because they carried the clear implication of a smiting "only to heal." (Isaiah 19:22) Crops cannot be gathered without first cutting the corn. Wine cannot be made without first crushing the grapes. Both activities appear as destruction when they are really fulfillment; and John uses these two harvest symbols to emphasize the real purpose of the seven plagues.

A being appears in heaven having a sharp sickle in his hand. He thrusts it into the earth and reaps, "for the harvest of the earth is ripe." (Rev. 14:15) Another being appears in heaven, "he also having a sharp sickle" (Rev. 14:17) and gathers the grapes of the earth to be crushed in the winepress of God. The juice of these grapes does not appear as wine but as blood. For the winepress is being trodden "outside the city." (Rev. 14:20) This is the holy city, the city of the awareness of God. Those who are "outside the city" do not realize that nothing is being destroyed except ignorance, and to them the crushing of the grapes appears as destruction rather than as fulfillment.

Then the seven angels make their appearance, carrying the seven vials that are filled with the seven plagues.

Again the Revelator pauses to emphasize the fact that these seven plagues have no effect whatever on those who have achieved "victory over the beast." (Rev. 15:2) Those who refuse to honor the beast have learned a new song, "the song of Moses, the servant of God, and the song of the Lamb." (Rev. 15:3) They have learned what Moses discovered when he gave to God the name of I AM (Exodus 3:14) and what Jesus meant when he said, "I am in union with my Father." (John 14:20) In whatever form the world may appear to them, they have learned to give it its true name. "Great and marvellous are thy works, Lord God Almighty . . . for thou only art holy." (Rev. 15:3–4)

The reason for the seven plagues is to make anything short of this full acknowledgment of God impossible. All that suffers under these seven plagues is ignorance concerning God. All that is destroyed is destruction. Therefore, in John's symbolism, it is angels who bring the plagues, each angel clothed in white linen and girdled with gold.

As soon as the vials holding the seven plagues have been given to the angels, "the temple was filled with smoke from the glory of God and from his power; and no man was able to enter into the temple, till the seven plagues of the seven angels were fulfilled." (Rev. 15:8)

The apparent peace of compromise can exist no longer. There will no longer be occasional entrances into "the temple," occasional moments of honoring the allness of God with life lived in the old way the rest of the time. No longer is it possible to make a compromise, trying to live part of the time in the kingdom of God and part of the time in the kingdom of the deceiver.

The purpose of the vials is to secure perfect acknowledgment of God, but this purpose is misunderstood by the men who have the mark of the beast upon them. They have identified themselves with what is being destroyed and therefore the plagues are a complete torment to them.

As has been said before, these "men" do not stand for any set of human beings. They stand for whatever honors material law as having real authority. They have tried to place themselves under the protection of the beast, they have worshiped it as a great power, and therefore, they remain for the time being under its law. The plagues are designed to force them away from their ignorance; and as long as they cling to this ignorance the plagues are a torment to them.

The contents of the first vial appear as disease, "a grievous sore upon the men which had the mark of the beast and upon them which worshipped his image." (Rev. 16:2) The second vial appears as blood upon the sea, the third as blood upon the rivers, and the fourth as overpowering heat from the sun. "Men were scorched with great heat, and blasphemed the name of God, which hath power over these plagues; and they repented not to give him glory." (Rev. 16:9)

The next vial is poured, not upon the earth but directly upon the kingdom of the beast—that is, upon its assumption of power and authority. At once "his kingdom was full of darkness." (Rev. 16:10) It has always been full of darkness, but only now is that fact becoming realized in the growing light of the kingdom of God. Yet still ignorance clings to what is familiar and "blasphemed the God of heaven because of their pains." (Rev. 16:11)

The sixth vial is poured out upon "the great river Euphrates." (Rev. 16:12) The Euphrates was historically the source and support of the mercantile wealth of the great city of Babylon, which was strategically located on its banks. In the Book of Revelation "Babylon" is used symbolically for what John calls love of the world, and the Euphrates is what supports the temptation of Babylon. When the sixth vial is poured out upon the Euphrates the river dries up.

The kingdom of the beast is dark and shaken, and it has lost the source that feeds one of its temptations. The dragon and his two delegates rouse themselves to protect the sovereignty they are in danger of losing, and they fight for it in the only way they know. Since they are deceivers, they continue with their attempt to deceive. "And I saw three unclean spirits like frogs come out of the mouth of the dragon, and out of the mouth of the beast, and out of the mouth of the false prophet." (Rev. 16:13)

This talk that comes out of the mouth of the dragon and his delegates has the power of seeming real to whoever believes in it. The frogs "are the spirits of devils, working miracles." (Rev. 16:14) They are capable of imitating the power of God and of thus securing belief for themselves and their originators.

These talking devils claim the power of uniting everything on earth to do battle against God. They "go forth unto the kings of the earth and of the whole world, to gather them to the battle of that great day of God Almighty." (Rev. 16:14)

Here the Revelator pauses to describe the nature of the battle on "that great day" when the spirit of truth meets the spirit of deceit: "Behold, I come as a thief. Blessed is he that watcheth." (Rev. 16:15) A thief comes as something to be feared, and in the darkest part of the night. It was in this way that Jacob's adversary came to him the night he earned for himself the name of Israel. The ability to recognize the identity of the "thief" that comes in the night takes persistent and consecrated effort; but there is no other way of being worthy of the title of Israel.

The talking devils fulfill their function and succeed in gathering together all the kings of the earth to make war against God. They gather them together "into a place called in the Hebrew tongue Armageddon." (Rev. 16:16)

Armageddon in Hebrew means "the mountains of Megiddo." It was near these mountains, according to the Book of Judges, that a battle was fought between the overlords of the district, the Canaanites, and the outnumbered, unarmed tribes of Israel. The Israelites won. The song of victory that was composed after the battle had for its theme, "The Lord made me have dominion over the mighty," (Judges 5:13) and it is this spirit that the Revelator is evoking in his symbolical use of the word Armageddon.

The final battle is not yet begun, but the work of the vials of judgment is over. The contents of the seventh vial are emptied, not on the earth but "into the air; and there came a great voice out of the temple of heaven, from the throne, saying, 'It is done.'" (Rev. 16:17)

It is "done" because the victory could not be achieved if there really existed a power apart from God that could deny the fact that God is all. The apparent existence of such a power is not a fact but only a deception; and this deception, which is based on ignorance, is being overcome by knowledge of God.

The acknowledgment that "It is done" precipitates another earthquake. "There has never been such an earthquake since man first existed upon the earth, it was so great." (Rev. 16:18) The whole of the former way of living is overturned, once it is acknowledged literally that God is all.

This acknowledgment is not something that can be used to make it possible to continue in the old way of living, merely curing it of its fears and diseases and making it as comfortable an experience as possible. Knowledge of God destroys the old way of life entirely. "He is the true God and eternal life," (I John 5:20) and apart from him there is no life at all.

Nevertheless, there is nothing of which the human mind is so terrified as the inability to make some kind of a compromise between the old way of life and the new. Although it is well aware of the truth of Jesus' statement that no man can serve two masters, it still wants to go on living in two worlds at once.

This point of view is only too anxious to proclaim the allness of God whenever it finds itself threatened by lack or disease or death. But the rest of the time it is quite willing to rest comfortably in the world it has always known, enjoying the health it has acquired through obedience to the laws of hygiene, the money it has earned through its own cleverness, the wisdom it has acquired through its own intelligence. These are all aspects of finity, of the belief of separation from the Father, but since they are pleasant aspects it is difficult not to cling to them.

This is the temptation that now makes its appearance in the Book of Revelation under the symbol of Babylon. It is the same temptation that John elsewhere calls love of the world. "Do not love the world or what is in the world. If anyone loves the world, there is no love of the Father in his heart, for all that there is in the world, the things that our physical nature and our eyes crave and the proud display of life—these do not come from the Father, but from the world; and the world and its cravings is passing away, but whoever does the will of God will endure forever." (I John 2:15–17)

John calls this temptation a city, because a city is habitually his symbol for a state of mind. And he calls the city Babylon because in both the Old and the New Testaments the capital city of Babylonia had become an accepted symbol for the temptation exerted by the things of the world.

Babylon is the quality that makes it extremely difficult to follow the truth with a whole heart and a whole mind, even at this stage of the warfare when the truth has been both revealed and understood. It represents the enormous pull earthward that John calls love of the world, and the temptation is a very strong one—"drunken with the blood of the saints." (Rev. 17:6)

This was the temptation that Jesus faced at the beginning of his ministry, the temptation to indulge in a compromise. "The devil took him to a very high mountain, and he showed him all the kingdoms of the world and their splendor, and said to him, 'I will give all this to you.'" (Matt. 4:8–9) The belief that finity had anything whatever to offer him was a temptation to which Jesus himself paid no attention. "Begone, Satan! For the Scripture says, 'You must do homage to the Lord your God, and worship him alone.'" (Matt. 4:10)

The answer that Jesus gave was the one he expected every follower of his to give also. Whoever sets out on "the way that leads to life" must be victorious "just as I have been victorious." (Rev. 3:21) And there can be no final victory—no real awareness of union with the Father—until the love of the world symbolized by Babylon is destroyed.

Babylon is first presented in the Book of Revelation as a woman. John is using here the symbol of the harlot that appears so often in Old Testament literature as a symbol of unfaithfulness to God.

The woman is seated on the beast; for it is the beast—the belief in a world that is not God's world—that gives Babylon authority. And the woman is exceedingly beautiful and desirable, "arrayed in purple and scarlet, and decked with gold and precious stones and pearls." (Rev. 17:4)

The mountain that appears in Matthew as the place of temptation becomes "seven mountains on which the woman sitteth." (Rev. 17:9) And the "kingdoms of the world" that the devil offers as a temptation in Matthew are personified in the Book of Revelation as "seven kings." (Rev. 17:10)

The seven kings do not rule simultaneously in Babylon, since what is a strong temptation at one stage of an individual's development has no effect upon him at another. But by this stage of the warfare, the rule of the seven kings is almost over. "Five are fallen, and one is, and the other is not yet come." (Rev. 17:10)

The beast himself is one of the temptations that rule in Babylon. "He is the eighth, and is one of the seven, and is to go to destruction." (Rev. 17:11) For the beast is both the final temptation and the origin of all the other temptations. The kings are his "seven heads" (Rev. 17:7) and it is upon the beast that the harlot sits.

Along with the seven heads, the beast also has ten horns. These symbolize the complete concentration of the beast's power, and "receive power as kings one hour with the beast." (Rev. 17:12)

These horns unite in a common purpose, to give the whole of "their power and strength unto the beast." (Rev. 17:13) They have "one mind" (Rev. 17:13) for they represent the concentration of all the forces that deny the allness of God. Yet in spite of themselves they function to the glory of God. "For God has put it into their hearts to do his mind by having a common mind and giving up their authority to the beast until the words of God shall be fulfilled." (Rev. 17:17)

"They shall war against the Lamb, and the Lamb shall overcome them." (Rev. 17:14) That is, this concentration of power is reversed by the knowledge of God and seen for what it really is; and this reversal destroys the authority of Babylon. "The ten horns . . . shall hate the whore and shall make her desolate." (Rev. 17:16) For all things work together for good for those that love God, even the concentration of power that seems to be arrayed on the side of the beast.

The fall of Babylon is given in the ancient prophetic form of a "doom song" against the city. The wording of the song is a composite of the Doom Songs of Isaiah and Jeremiah against the original historical city of Babylon, combined with Ezekiel's beautiful dirge on the fall of maritime Tyre.

Babylon has been a great city, ruling over all the kings of the earth. The merchants have grown rich trading with her, and her position is impregnable in her own eyes. "I sit a queen, and am no widow, and shall see no sorrow." (Rev. 18:7) The list of merchandise in which she trades includes every commodity of value: "Merchandise of gold and silver and precious stones, and of pearls and fine linen . . . and of brass and iron . . . and wine and oil and fine flour and wheat, and cattle and sheep and horses and chariots and slaves and the souls of men." (Rev. 18:12–13)

The wording of the final doom against Babylon, however, does not resemble the phrases of the prophets when they wrote of Babylon and Tyre. The phrase instead is the one that Jeremiah used three times, each time when he was prophesying the end of the city of Jerusalem. (Jeremiah 7:34, 16:9, 25:10; Rev. 18:23)

In his own day Jeremiah was fighting the conviction of the citizens that the actual physical city of Jerusalem was so good and so holy that nothing could destroy it. The point that Jeremiah was making in his prophecy against the city of Jerusalem is that nothing can be trusted, so long as it is apart from God, no matter how good it appears to be.

By borrowing his wording from Jeremiah, John makes it clear that Babylon does not symbolize merely the temptation of finite evil. It also stands for the much more subtle and effective temptation of finite good. It was this temptation that Jesus rejected when he said, "Why do you call me good? No one is good but God himself." (Luke 18:19) For to agree that any quality can somehow be maintained separately from God is to deny that God is all.

Jerusalem seemed very safe and admirable to its inhabitants in the days of Jeremiah, but Jeremiah knew that this safety was based on a misunderstanding.[6] He prophesied that the holy city would fall; and it fell. And Babylon falls likewise.

Jeremiah was writing of a physical city, one that was eventually conquered by a physical army. The Revelator is writing of a state of mind. Only one thing can destroy the city of which John is writing: the refusal to be tempted by it any longer. Love of the world has to be abandoned entirely, for it can never be combined with love of God.

Once the temptation of Babylon is rejected, it is suddenly found that everything that was valued in the city does not exist in it at all. All delight is vanished out of Babylon, "the voice of harpers and musicians, and of pipers and trumpeters." (Rev. 18:22) The pleasure of successful achievement is no longer in Babylon; "no craftsman, of whatsoever craft, shall be found any more in thee." (Rev. 18:22) The city will no longer be looked to as a source of supply, for the sound of the millstone, which was the instrument used for grinding corn, "shall be heard no more at all in thee." (Rev. 18:22)

No longer will the city be trusted to give light. "The light of a candle shall shine no more at all in thee." (Rev. 18:23) And no more will the city be believed in as the home of either joy or completeness. "The voice of the bridegroom and the voice of the bride shall be

---

[6] See Chapter 10 of *The Search for God* for a full discussion of Jeremiah's attitude towards Jerusalem.

heard no more at all in thee." (Rev. 18:23) For the belief that all these things could be found in Babylon was never true. By her "sorceries were all the nations deceived" (Rev. 18:23) and the deception is now ended.

It is not until the light vanishes out of Babylon that the real light becomes visible; then it is found that nothing has been lost and everything has been fulfilled. Nothing is lost through the destruction of Babylon. All things are now merely released from the bondage of the mistaken belief that they ever were in Babylon—that is, that they ever existed as separate from God. When John describes, in the seventh vision, the new, perfect city that finally appears, it is not a "candle" that lights it, but the glory of God. (Rev. 21:23)

The city of God has not yet appeared, but the joyfulness that belongs to it is already evident. "The Lord our God, the Almighty, now reigns. Let us be glad and triumphant and give him glory, for the marriage of the Lamb has come and his bride hath made herself ready." (Rev. 19:6–7)

Marriage as the symbol of union with God is a familiar symbol in both the Old and the New Testaments. The special point to be noticed about John's use of the symbol is the way he describes the bride. She is "arrayed in fine linen, clean and white; for the fine linen is the righteousness of the saints." (Rev. 19:8)

The saints, as has been said before, stand for the highest aspect of human endeavor; and up to this point they have been unsuccessful. The saints have been slain under the altar, they have failed to conquer the beast, they have died in Babylon. But now that Babylon has been destroyed, a change comes over the dogged, ineffective warfare of the "saints." For the destruction of Babylon means the destruction of trying to maintain anything separate from God, and one of the things that has been maintained is human endeavor.

From now on, the highest aspect of human endeavor consists in the abandonment of human endeavor. It consists in acknowledging that all activity, all responsibility and all authority belong only to God. It is not human endeavor that enforces the power of God. What enforces it is the fact that it is already so.

This is "the spirit of truth that comes from the Father." (John 15:26) It is this that is both the warrior and the victor. The only obligation of the individual is to be willing to acknowledge the spirit of truth, the fact that it is already so.

THE SIXTH VISION

The sixth vision deals with the final warfare between the spirit of truth and the spirit of deceit.

"And I saw heaven opened, and behold a white horse. And he that sat upon him was called faithful and true, and in righteousness he doth judge and make war. His eyes were as a flame of fire, and on his head were many crowns . . . and his name is called the Word of God." (Rev. 19:11–13)

It will be remembered that a rider on a white horse made an appearance in the second vision, when the first of the seals was opened. Here the rider symbolized the expectation of victory that occurs at the very beginning of the warfare, the untried confidence that has met no adversary. But now the rider on the white horse symbolizes not the shadow of victory but its substance. On his head are "many crowns." (Rev. 19:12)

In the long warfare against varying aspects of deceit, the individual has discovered that the victory is not his. The victory belongs to the spirit of truth. The "saints" have learned to follow the Word of God instead of trying to do the work themselves; or, to use John's symbolism, they follow the rider on the white horse instead of trying to ride alone. Therefore, they are now mounted on the white horses that symbolize victory. They are the armies of heaven. Having learned to acknowledge the truth, they are now willing to let the truth do its own work.

Now that the whole warfare against the dragon has been concentrated under the banner of the Word of God, a similar concentration takes place among the forces that are operating on the other side. "I saw the beast, and the kings of the earth and their armies, gathered together to make war against him that sat on the horse and against his army." (Rev. 19:19)

Now that God has been acknowledged to be the whole of manifestation, the beast is seen to be the result of a lie about manifestation; and through the spirit of truth this deception is believed in no longer. "The beast was taken, and with him the false prophet that wrought miracles before him, with which he deceived them that had received the mark of the beast and them that worshiped his image. These both were cast alive into a lake of fire burning with brimstone." (Rev. 19:20)

The lake of fire is an image taken from the apocalypses and means total destruction. There is no power left in the beast and the false prophet, and they never appear again to deceive the earth.

"And the remnant were slain with the sword of him that sat upon the horse." (Rev. 19:21) This remnant refers to "the kings of the earth and their armies" who were led by the beast to make war against the Word of God. They were gathered together in the preceding vision by "spirits like frogs coming out of the mouth of the dragon, and out of the mouth of the beast, and out of the mouth of the false prophet." (Rev. 16:13) It is by a reversal of the same method that they are overcome, "slain with the sword of him that sat upon the horse, which sword proceeded out of his mouth." (Rev. 19:21) The authority that is evoked by the talking serpent is destroyed by the Word of God.

This is the end of the second warfare recorded in the Book of Revelation.

The first warfare took place "in heaven." Here the dragon was overcome by the birth of understanding and cast forever out of heaven. That is, he was no longer credited with being reality but was seen for what he was, a liar and the father of lies.

The dragon was not destroyed. He was cast down "to earth" and the purpose of the second warfare was to get him off the earth also. This was done by destroying the two delegates through which the dragon was able to manifest his power "on earth"—that is, visibly.

With the destruction of the beast and the false prophet, the dragon can manifest himself on earth no longer, since God is now known to include within himself the whole of manifestation.

After this second victory the dragon can no longer operate on earth; the earth is known to be the showing-forth of the glory of God. But the dragon himself still exists. He is the fundamental lie of separation from God, and this lie has not yet been destroyed but only disarmed.

The Revelator symbolizes this by the dragon being cast off the earth. "And I saw an angel come down from heaven, having the key of the bottomless pit and a great chain in his hand. And he laid hold on the dragon, that old serpent which is the Devil and Satan, and bound him a thousand years, and cast him into the bottomless pit, and shut him up and put a seal on him that he should deceive the nations no more." (Rev. 20:1–3)

From now on, the reign of the dragon is apparently over. He cannot manifest himself, for God is understood to be the only manifestation; and he cannot kill, for God is known to be the only life. The understanding of this is the Christ, and with it the saints reign on earth. "And I saw the souls of them . . . which had not worshiped the beast . . . and they lived and reigned with Christ a thousand years." (Rev. 20:4)

This "thousand years" is the familiar millennial kingdom of the Jewish apocalypses. John followed the framework of these apocalypses whenever it suited his purpose, and here he found the symbol a useful one. If the idea of a thousand years of reigning had not already become familiar through the writings of the period, John might have used any other period of time to carry the same meaning. Any number of years, that is, other than seven or twelve, the two numbers that symbolize completeness.

For the kingdom that the saints establish on earth is an incomplete kingdom. It is nothing more than an extension of the conviction expressed at the end of the first vision, before the real warfare has begun: "We shall reign on the earth." (Rev. 5:10) As long as there is something to be reigned over there is something separate from God, and in the idea that anything is separate from God lies the whole power of the dragon. Or, to use John's symbolism, the dragon has been cast out of heaven and has lost its authority on earth, but he is still waiting "in the pit."

Victory over the dragon's delegates has not meant victory over the dragon. As long as there is any sense of separation, any idea that there is something to be "reigned over" in order to maintain the kingdom of God upon earth, then the kingdom is precarious and incomplete and will end sooner or later. The phrase "a thousand years" is merely a symbol of this inevitable ending.

"When the thousand years are expired" (Rev. 20:7) the dragon comes up out of the pit. The lie that has its roots in the belief that the son is separate from the Father suddenly resumes its activity and no human effort to "reign" can stand against it. The "camp of the saints" (Rev. 20:9) is compassed about by the armies of the dragon and is helpless to defend itself.

Therefore, and this is the final phase of the warfare, human endeavor is abandoned forever. It implies separation and there is no separation, no necessity for warfare, no responsibility for victory. There is nothing to war against since God is all, nothing to guard against and nothing to conquer. "I am in union with my Father." (John 14:20)

This is the final victory, and it is symbolized by the Revelator with a picture of the complete destruction of everything that is unlike God. "The devil that deceived them was cast into the lake of fire and brimstone, where the beast and the false prophet are." (Rev. 20:10) John gives the standard apocalyptic formula for the end of the world, since the old way of looking at the world is now at an end forever. "Death and hell were cast into the lake of fire" (Rev. 20:14) and everything else that had no real existence—anything "not found written in the book of life" (Rev. 20:15)—was cast in with them.

This is the end of the warfare to find God, when the necessity for fighting is ended and the responsibility is over. It is the end of the old world and the beginning of a new one, and Paul described it once in a way that could not be bettered. "After that will come the end, when he shall turn over the kingdom to God his Father, bringing to an end all other government, authority and power ... And when everything is reduced in subjection to him, then the son himself will also become subject to him who has reduced everything to subjection to him; so that God may be all in all." (I Cor. 15:24, 28)

THE SEVENTH VISION

The seventh vision brings perfect peace.

"And I saw a new heaven and a new earth; for the first heaven and the first earth were passed away, and there was no more sea. And I, John, saw the holy city, the new Jerusalem, coming down from God out of heaven prepared as a bride adorned to meet her husband. And I heard a great voice out of heaven saying, 'Behold, the tabernacle of God is with men, and he will dwell with them, and they shall be his people, and God himself shall be with them and be their God. And God shall wipe away all tears from their eyes; and there shall be no more death, neither sorrow nor crying, neither shall there be any more pain.' " (Rev. 21:1-4) For all these things were born of a failure to understand God, and the failure is ended. "The former things are passed away." (Rev. 21:4)

This is the victory that was promised to the individual in the prologue to the Book of Revelation. It was promised in each of the messages to the seven churches, and now that it has been fulfilled the seven promises are grouped together and made one. "He that overcometh shall inherit all things; and I will be his God, and he shall be my son." (Rev. 21:7)

Anything that is unlike this union with the Father can no longer exist. "The fearful, and unbelieving, and the abominable, and murderers, and whoremongers, and sorcerers, and idolaters, and all liars" (Rev. 21:8) are cast into the lake of fire; that is, all fear and unbelief and pollution and death and adultery and deception and idolatry and lies are destroyed forever, along with the deceiver who gave them their power to exist.

There is no longer any warfare. The holy city is not like the armed camp of the previous vision, liable to attack at any moment. For the dragon is destroyed, and with him the belief in anything unlike God.

Nevertheless, it was this warfare and the victory that it finally produced that makes it possible to live in the city of God. Or, to use John's symbolism, it was one of the angels who brought the seven plagues who now shows the Revelator "that great city, the holy Jerusalem, descending out of heaven from God." (Rev. 21:10)

The warfare did not create the city, but it did create the ability to recognize its existence. The city did not need to be created. Being the truth, it had existed always. What has been created in the course of the long warfare is the ability of the individual to recognize the existence of the city, to see it "descending out of heaven from God, having the glory of God." (Rev. 21:10–11)

Jesus spoke of a continuing fact when he said, "The kingdom of God is within you." (Luke 17:21) But the discovery of the kingdom comes only through warfare. It is not until the individual is victorious over his belief in everything unlike God that he enters the kingdom of his presence. Nevertheless, no matter how long it may take for its presence to be acknowledged, nothing can alter the fact that the kingdom of God is a "continuing city." (Hebrews 13:14)

John has made this point clear throughout the whole of the Book of Revelation. In the course of the book he pauses again and again to show in pictures the glory that belongs to God, as much before the warfare has begun and in the thick of the conflict as when the holy city is actually manifest. The warfare is an apparent warfare only, since the adversary is not real. Reality does not change, and the kingdom of God is the kingdom of God always.

John's symbol for this kingdom is "that great city, the holy Jerusalem" (Rev. 21:10) and to describe the city he evokes all the symbols used by the Old Testament prophets to mean light and completeness and joy.

The radiance of the city is like clear crystal; the foundations are twelve precious stones and its gates twelve pearls. The city is of "pure gold, like clear glass" (Rev. 21:21) and all its dimensions are those that symbolize completeness.

Within the city is the river of life, "proceeding out of the throne of God" (Rev. 22:1) and it waters the tree of life, bearing twelve times twelve, whose leaves are for the healing of the nations. There is no temple in the city, for God is the only temple; and there is no need to illumine the city, for God is its only light.

The gates of the city are never closed and everything may freely enter in. Even the "kings of the earth" that once seemed to be fighting on the side of the beast now "bring their glory and honor into it." (Rev. 21:24) For God is all, and everything may be freely honored as his presence.

Yet, though the city is freely entered, it is guarded from anything unlike itself. "There shall no wise enter into it anything that defileth, nor anything that worketh abomination or maketh a lie." (Rev. 21:27) For truth has nothing to do with lies, and by its very nature it is perfectly protected from anything unlike itself.

With the picture of the holy city, the seventh vision of the Book of Revelation ends. The Way-shower has shown the way that leads to life, and "blessed is he that keepeth the sayings of the prophecy of this book." (Rev. 22:7)

There remains an epilogue, to balance the prologue with which the Book of Revelation opened. In the epilogue, John represents himself as trying to worship the man who gave him the contents of the book. He falls at his feet to give him honor and is instantly checked. "See that thou do it not; for I am thy fellow servant, and of thy brethren the prophets, and of them which keep the sayings of this book. Worship God." (Rev. 22:9)

The contents of the book are free to anyone capable of accepting them. "Whosoever will, let him take the water of life freely." (Rev. 22:17) But not a word is to be added to the message, and not a word is to be taken away. Then, after the warning, a blessing is given.

"The grace of our Lord Jesus Christ be with you all. Amen." (Rev. 22:21) This ends the Book of Revelation, the chart of the "way that leads to life."

In some respects the Book of Revelation is very similar to the discourse of the Last Supper. It was given for the same purpose: "I have told you all this so that you may have the happiness I have had and your happiness may be complete." (John 15:11) It was told by the same method, "in figurative language." (John 16:25) And it was recorded by the same man.

John was the one disciple who had proved himself capable of remembering what Jesus said the night of the Last Supper, and it was therefore John who was permitted to write the Book of Revelation. He was the one disciple who knew that the warfare was between "the spirit of truth and the spirit of deceit" (I John 4:6) and he had already stated his conviction that the warfare could have only one ending:

> We know that we are the children of God, while the whole world is under the power of the evil one. And we know that the son of God has come and has given us power to recognize him who is true, through his son, Jesus Christ. He is the true God and eternal life. Dear children, keep away from idols. (1 John 5:19–21)

If this passage from one of John's letters is translated into he language he uses in the Book of Revelation, it becomes a condensed version of the whole action of the book.

> We know that we are the sons of God, even though the whole world is being deceived by the dragon. And we know that Jesus brought us the full truth about God and the ability to recognize his holy city. He is the true God and he is eternal life. Dear children, do not honor that which is unreal.

—————·>‹‹·——————

GLOSSARY OF TERMS
USED IN THE
BOOK OF REVELATION

earth: visible outward manifestation.

city: a state of mind. There are three in the Book of Revelation.

> 1. The city in which the two witnesses are slain—symbolizing unbelief.
>
> 2. Babylon—symbolizing love of the world.
>
> 3. Jerusalem—symbolizing the realization of the presence of God.

saints: the highest and holiest aspect of human endeavor.

Christ: the full understanding of God.

birth of the man child: birth of the individual's understanding of God.

dragon: the deceiver. The basic lie of separation which claims to be able to produce a world that is not God's world.

beast: the belief in matter.

false prophet: the belief in the power of mind over matter.

seal: protection.

horns: power.

lamb: historically, the sacrifice offered by the high priest on the Day of Atonement. Used to symbolize Jesus, who through the crucifixion proved his at-one-ment with the Father. Also used by extension to symbolize the Christ, the complete understanding of God that Jesus possessed.

white: the symbol of purity.

rider on a white horse: the symbol of victory.

earthquake: an overturning of what has formerly been considered secure.

kings of the earth: anything that has been given authority

temple: the awareness of the fact that God is all.

fire: purification; light appearing as destruction.

idols: the belief in any power apart from God.

Israel: literally "striver with God." That which says to whatever appears, "I will not let you go unless you bless me." (Genesis 32:26)

seven: completeness; used either for good or evil.

twelve: holy completeness.

six: incompleteness; the number that falls just short of seven.

three and a half: a period of testing.